Bringing Forth the
Sons of God

Bringing Forth the Sons of God

❖

Walking in Spiritual Maturity

Reverend Audrey Drummonds

iUniverse, Inc.
New York Lincoln Shanghai

Bringing Forth the Sons of God
Walking in Spiritual Maturity

All Rights Reserved © 2004 by Audrey Drummonds

No part of this book may be reproduced or transmitted in any form or by any means, graphic, electronic, or mechanical, including photocopying, recording, taping, or by any information storage retrieval system, without the written permission of the publisher.

iUniverse, Inc.

For information address:
iUniverse, Inc.
2021 Pine Lake Road, Suite 100
Lincoln, NE 68512
www.iuniverse.com

Unless otherwise noted in the text, all Scriptures have been taken from the King James Version Hebrew-Greek Key Study Bible, copyright 1984 and 1991, Sprios Zodhiate and AMG International, Inc. d/b/a AMG Publishers

ISBN: 0-595-31244-6 (pbk)
ISBN: 0-595-66283-8 (cloth)

Printed in the United States of America

"For it became him, for whom are all things, and by whom are all things, in bringing many sons unto glory, to make the captain of their salvation perfect through sufferings."
(Hebrews 2:10)

"We know that we have passed from death unto life, because we love the brethren."
(1 John 3:17)

"Anyone who does not love is as good as dead."
Joyce Meyer

"EGO= edging God out. The Ego's greatest fear is that you will come to know God, and that you are god, and He is within you."
Dr. Wayne W. Dyer

Contents

Introduction		ix
CHAPTER 1	Traditional Teachings	1
CHAPTER 2	Who is God to You?	7
CHAPTER 3	Hear the Word of the Lord	17
CHAPTER 4	Heaven is the Substance of Reality	25
CHAPTER 5	Do We Have Two Minds?	39
CHAPTER 6	God's Habitation in You	47
CHAPTER 7	The Return of Christ	57
CHAPTER 8	Bringing Forth the Sons of God	69
CHAPTER 9	Being Transformed into His Image	75
APPENDIX	Scriptures for References	85

Introduction

When writing a book, one must ponder how to bring their audience to an understanding of the author's position or mindset. My thoughts for this book came from an in-depth hunger and longing to KNOW God according to what the Holy Spirit has taught me through the Scriptures, based on my personal experience of being healed from an incurable disease, and my life experiences of many trials and tribulations.

Though I was raised in the "Christian church," I found myself with many questions in my search for the answers to my life's situations that the denominational training I was receiving wasn't able to give to my satisfaction. For this reason, other than the Scriptures, the resources I have limited myself to are *Strong's Concordance*, a Hebrew-Greek Dictionary, and the Old and New Testament Lexicon. I have stayed away from commentaries to help me stay focused on allowing the Holy Spirit to be the teacher of this book. I have also tried to limit the sharing of my personal experiences to reduce the attention to myself. Through negative encounters of my life, I have been able to find love, hope, and peace that were applied while in the midst of the circumstances. This has enabled me to become an overcomer in Christ Jesus, which is what gave me the material to write this book. Seeing Scriptures through the eyes of love will bring to the reader a fresh awakening from denominational religion into the beauty and wonder of how much their Heavenly Father loves them.

The word "sons" used in the title and throughout the book is not referring to gender of male or female, but is used in context with Scripture based on the difference between children of God, and those that are the mature body of Christ known as "sons." In the book of Genesis we are told that Adam was created in the image of God, both male and female. If Scripture can refer to all believers, male and female, as the "bride of Christ," we can also consider Scripture referring to males and females as being "sons" of God. As children of God, we are in a stage of learning, but as "sons" of God we should be at a stage of spiritual growth that when others see us they see the Father because of the maturity of understanding who their Heavenly Father is.

Scripture tells us, "In the beginning was the Word, and the Word was with God, and the Word was God" (John 1:1). According to this Scripture, God is the Word. It isn't God over "here" and the Scriptures over "there." It also tells us that the Word is Jesus. The Word was with God, and the Word is God. God is Spirit and eternal. He is ALL light and ALL life. He has no darkness and no death. Therefore, the Word (Jesus/Scripture) must also be the same. God is taken out and religion is filled in when we use the Word of the Lord for self-desires, lacing it with judgment and condemnation.

When God gave us the Scripture writings, they were written through a Jewish mindset. Even though the New Testament was written in Greek, Jesus and the disciples spoke and thought with a Jewish mind. The major difference between the Greek and Jewish mindset is that the Greeks see Scripture as philosophical, and the

Jewish understanding of the Scriptures is as a personal conversation with God.

The Greeks believe the natural mind must make sense of the things of God. They also believe that the more education a person has in theology and philosophy, the greater chance he will have in understanding the Word. The Greek uses these means in trying to interpret what God is saying. The Greek mindset may acknowledge the existence of the Holy Spirit, but it puts aside the fact that it IS the Holy Spirit who reveals the mysteries of God. Today we know that the Holy Spirit does not require anyone to have a college degree to bring forth revelation knowledge.

In contrast, the Hebrew mind asks, "What is God saying to you, and what are YOU going to do with it?" The Hebrew mind gives respect to the fact that wisdom of the Word brings life and light to different parts of the body in different ways. It is a walk of faith to believe there is only one Holy Spirit and one God. Even though there are many members of one body, it is only the blood of Jesus, the Word, which gives life to the many members. This kind of faith declares that it is the responsibility of the Holy Spirit to bring unity to the body.

This Hebrew mindset is the perspective from which I have chosen to share thoughts, which aim to bring unity and light to the body of Christ. I do not expect the reader to have a full understanding of what is written in this book, nor do I expect full agreement with my thoughts and research. My goal is to stir the spirit of the reader to examine their Christian views and encourage the allowance of the Holy Spirit to be the author and finisher of their faith in the Lord Jesus Christ, versus letting doctrinal teachings being the source of revelation.

The teachings in this book have been compiled from essays written for our website, www.InteriorCoveringsMinistry.org. The website offers a wonderful opportunity to reach people around the world with the Good News of the Gospel of Jesus Christ. However, without a hard copy of the material, it is difficult for the reader to ponder the teachings and/or do an in-depth study. We have therefore put some of the teachings into book form. All proceeds received from the sale of this book are given to Interior Coverings Ministry, a nonprofit organization, to be used for outreach missions furthering the Kingdom of God. I encourage the use of highlighters, underlining, and note taking in the margins as the Holy Spirit stirs your inner being.

Acknowledgments

I would like to say thank you to my husband, Ron, and my children, Greg, Ashley, and Michael. They have not always understood and agreed with my writings, but they have encouraged me with their love and support, allowing the fruit of His Holy Spirit to be manifested. I would like to also give thanks to a few very special people in my life for making this book possible. Janet Acker, my editor and dear friend, has stirred the Word in me with her questions and passion for truth. Janet Bassett is my publisher for ICM newsletters and lifelong friend who has helped me search out love and life. Linda Goldstein has been my supporter and encourager by being a STAR, shining brightly for our Heavenly Father. My parents, Frank and Lydia Thomas, have always lifted me up to go beyond what I thought possible. Dr. Joanne Bunce, my inspiration and mentor, has encouraged me to believe in myself, trust the voice of the Holy Spirit in me, and to always keep a teachable spirit ready to go beyond the realm of denominational belief into knowing my Heavenly Father as Truth, Light, Life, and Love.

1

Traditional Teachings

We know that God is Spirit without a form or body. He is God to Himself; indefinable, invisible, eternal, having no boundaries, and in Him there is no darkness. When He takes on a form, it is to reproduce Him.

In the book of Genesis, we read in Chapter 1, Verse 26, a conversation which took place that is traditionally taught to be Jesus, the Holy Ghost, and the Father speaking to one another. *"And God said, 'Let us make man in our image, after our likeness: and let them have dominion over the fish of the sea, and over the fowl of the air, and over the cattle, and over all the earth, and over every creeping thing that creepeth upon the earth.'"* It is often implied that they were bored, and so they decided to create an "Adam" who turned out to be a rebellious freak. Adam failed because he did exactly what God told him not to do. His failure implies that God goofed in His perfect plan, and brought Jesus into the picture as plan B. Included with this traditional concept is that the serpent was smarter than God and fooled both God and Adam from the beginning. Supposedly, man was given a choice to be a free moral agent, and failed as if God wasn't really involved. As silly as this may sound with a few "thee's," "thou's," and "thus," it is very much what many Christian leaders believe and teach today. If man really did fail and is a disappointment to God, what has happened to the image of God? Did man "fall"...yes! Does God know all...yes! Did God know the fall of man would happen before it happened...yes! Is God absolute...yes!

Scripture tells us the Lamb of God was slain *BEFORE* the foundations of the world (Rev.13:8). God took care of the problem before there was a problem. He created the victory before the fight, and He declared the End before the Beginning. In II Timothy 1:9-10 we read, *"Who hath saved us, and called us with a holy calling, not according to our works, but according to his own purpose and grace, which was given us in Christ Jesus before the world began, but is NOW made manifest by the appearing of our Savior Jesus Christ, who hath abolished death, and hath brought life and immortality to light through the gospel."* God finishes first, and then manifests what He starts. He is Spirit and doesn't need to dwell in time going from point A to point B. God knew the end before He started anything and executed His plan to perfection. There had to be a first Adam, because the last Adam had already been slain for the fall of the first. The last Adam (Jesus) was the finished, but it took the first Adam to reveal the process of the beginning. The last Adam came forth to show the manifestation of the finished work from the first to the last. The growth, the developing, and the maturing had to take place to bring forth the image of God, the Sons of God.

Every commandment and revelation of the Word of God causes more of His character, His nature, and His identity to be released and manifested in us. The commandments that say, "Thou shall not" are not so God can judge with legalism, but so that He will be revealed in us showing forth His nature and likeness out of us. It is not a life of do's and don'ts, but a life where God, who is already ALL in us, reveals this reality to us by the Holy Spirit unveiling our true identity. When truth is manifested through us there is no darkness possible.

Hebrews 8:10-12 reads, *"For this is the covenant that I will make with the house of Israel after those days, saith the Lord; I will put my laws into their minds, and write them in their hearts: and I will be to them a God, and they shall be to me a people: and they shall not teach every man his neighbor, and every man his brother, saying, know the Lord: for ALL shall know me, from the least to the greatest. For I will be merciful to their unrighteousness, and their sins and their iniquities will I remember no more."*

Galatians 1:15-16 reads, *"But when it pleased God, who separated me from my mother's womb, and called me by his grace to reveal his Son in me that I might preach him among the heathen; immediately I conferred not with flesh and blood."*

God has given us His name and nature, but for the likeness of God to come forth within us we must experience the reality of heaven now as substance versus the "someday" when we get to heaven. When we carry the mindset of waiting till we "cross over" to receive the fullness of our inheritance we are walking in a self-centered mentality that says, "What is my reward?" versus "What can I give to others?" Most of what we call Christianity is a display of being too "chicken" and lukewarm to be willing to go through the training and experience or trials and tribulations so that our Father will be glorified today as a testimony of His goodness and love to the world. *"For God so loved the world that He gave His only Son…"* John 3:16.

What does it mean to take each day as the day of the Lord's to glorify the Father? First, we should keep our understanding on the fact that we are alive today to glorify Him, not ourselves. Then, when God brings people across your path it is for a reason that the Holy Spirit has set before you to honor the Father. We should first look upon others with the eyes of Jesus, our husband, full of compassion, love, and mercy, letting no condemnation or judgment come forth. We should look within their heart, evaluate their words, and take note of what is going on in their life with a willingness to take their burdens upon ourselves and declare the peace of God upon them. Our calling as Christians is to be the intercessor, ambassador of Christ, and priest for that moment of time in their lives. They may not be able to see the fullness of hope in their circumstance, but by OUR faith and intercession given to us by the Holy Spirit, we can take their burdens upon ourselves so His grace and mercy will be manifested in their situation, and our Heavenly Father will be glorified.

This is not a hit and miss magical potion. It is a declaration of the work of the Son of God being manifested in the life of a Christ One. We are declaring our identity with the full power and authority given to us as our inheritance, as the bride of Christ, to be received *now* while in our flesh. We can walk and make this declaration for others only if we truly have the intimacy of knowing the fullness of what Jesus accomplished on the cross.

In marriage, the bride takes on the name of her husband. With that name is given the power and authority to do the husband's business. We are children of God. When we have reached a level of maturity, we recognize that our purpose here on this earth is to do our Father's business. Since we are married to the Son, and are joint heirs with Him, we recognize that as He is Jesus Christ the Lord, we are *(your name)* Christ the Lord/Lady. He is KING of kings, and LORD of lords, that God may be ALL in ALL, (I Corinthians 15:28), *"And when all things shall be subdued unto him, then shall the son also himself be subject unto him that put all things under him, that God may be all in all."*

Our husband, Jesus Christ, is sitting at the right hand of God the Father (Colossians 3:1). He is the Father of Jesus and He is our Father according to John 20:17. The act of sitting is resting which declares a completed work. They are sitting at the great white throne of judgment, or the seat of unconditional love, mercy, and forgiveness. This takes us to the end of the Bible in Revelation, Chapters 20, 21, and 22. Since there is no beginning and no ending with God, what we call the end of the book is really taking us back to Genesis 1:1, *"In the beginning God."* God is Love; God is Light; and God is Life. He is eternal. In the beginning we have unconditional Love, Life, and Light with no time. In the end we have the same. Jesus is the Alpha and Omega; He is the first and the last of all things (Revelation 1:10). A little further on in this same chapter we read in Verse 17-18, *"Fear not; I am the first and the last: I am he that liveth, and was dead; and behold, I am alive forevermore, Amen; and have the keys of hell and of death."*

As the bride of Jesus Christ, and as His body, the world should be seeing love, life, and light in us. This can only happen when we have an intimate relationship with our beloved, as a husband and wife experience in intercourse. Our true identity, as sons of God, and purpose in this world can be manifested as we acknowledge that His seed and blood flow through us because of the finished work on Calvary two thousand years ago. When He died, we died, and we He rose from the dead, we rose, and we are now seated with Him in heavenly places to rule and reign with Him.

2

Who is God to You?

When you hear the word God what kind of connection do you see yourself having with "God?" We can say according to Scripture that God is Love (1 John 4:8 and 16), God is Light (1 John 1:5), God is Life (John 11:25), and that God is all in all (Colossians 3:11). We know that God is Spirit, and not tangible to our understanding. When we know God as described above we are in the midst of the place called the Holy of Holies, yet we cannot get there with our natural understanding. This place is the inner court referred to in the Old Testament, where the High Priest entered once a year. He went into the presence of God on this earth. However, only the High Priest was able to have this interaction with God. For everyone else, their relationship came through the experience of the High Priest. Now, we can experience the High Priest's interaction with God on a daily basis.

Now, walk with me to the word "Father." What do we think of? First of all, we know that it takes a seed planted in a womb, or in a darkened place, because father means there must be children of the same bloodline that carries his DNA. A father is tangible.

Genesis 1:26 says, *"Let us make man in our image."* Our Heavenly Father, God, is not one that says, "Do as I say, but don't do as I do."

When He created Adam (mankind), he did not create things, but children in His image. The comparison of Scriptures in Genesis 5:1-2 and Luke 3:38 show us that both male and female were recognized as "Adam," and "Adam" was recognized as a son of God in both Old and New Testaments. When Adam rebelled against our Father he did not lose his identity of being a Son of God, and he didn't lose his dominion or authority over the earth. What he lost was his ability to know our Father in his identity as a Son of God. He altered the ability he had to "Be" the Son of God by trying to please his Father. This created a "works" relationship instead of one based on love.

In Romans 5:12-21, we read about the contrast between Adam and Jesus Christ. Our Father could not be calling anyone a sinner or else he would be nullifying the finished work of the cross. The word sinner means "one who sins," or "one who has taken the action of sinning." It is not an identity name, anymore than the words "stupid," "adulterer," or "thief" are the names of a person's genealogy. We need to reconsider Adam's bloodline, or ours, with how God called Adam His son, and Jesus His Son from the same genealogy in Luke, Chapter 3. Scripture does not tell us that God called man a sinner based on bloodline identity, but to distinguish the action man engaged in that caused separation from God. The work of the cross is a finished work that Jesus completed to bring our relationship as the sons of God back into unity with our Father so that His glory may shine.

Think about this—if our children are involved with smoking, drinking alcohol, teenage sex/or pregnancy, stealing, robbery, listening to secular music, involved with homosexuality, doing drugs, or even cursing us as parents, do we disown our children when they are doing any or all of these things? Not if we have unconditional love for them. No matter what rebellious action our children can be a part of, we will always be their father or mother because of the bloodline and DNA. Our children will have to deal with the consequences of their actions, or sin, but they cannot lose their identity as our children because of the DNA in their blood. What is interesting is many churches that are supposed to be our spiritual families would disown their members if they were involved with any of the above. Jesus could not function with all power and authority if He carried the blood of the Father, and His body, the church, carried the blood of what we call a sinner. The Life of the flesh, or our eternal salvation, comes from His blood (Leviticus 17:14).

Luke 1:35 tells us that Jesus became a "thing" so we don't have to be a "thing" anymore. The word human is a "thing" that does not belong. God created sons and beasts in Genesis, Chapters 1 and 2. Man created the word and gave life to it. Did you know the word "human" is not in the Scriptures? It is important for us to learn the ways of our Father with the mind of Christ versus the mind of a human in order to come into His presence in the Holy of Holies.

The power of life and death comes from our words (Proverbs 18:21), but when our words are of a righteous man, Jesus, they are a well of Life (Proverbs 10:11). This word "Life" comes from the Hebrew word "chay" meaning to live in wholeness and forever. The Hebrews viewed man holistically: your body, mind, and soul were a unified whole. Life was associated with health, prosperity, and vitality, which came from God. It was permissible to eat from the Tree of Life in the Garden of Eden, but not from the Tree of Knowledge of good and evil. Whether the knowledge was good or evil the end result would still be the same, eventually bringing forth death. The Tree of Life had no death.

This may be a good stopping place to think about what has just been discussed.

Now, let us go to the words "son" and "child" from a biblical understanding. The concept of adoption the Bible talks about is different than what we think of in America. Adoption to us is taking in a stranger and giving them our name. We use this concept with Christianity by taking in a sinner/gentile and calling them a Christian because they chose to be a part of the family of God. This way of thinking is Old Testament religion. The Jews saw themselves as the children of God. This family of God was kept in order by rules and rituals, or dos and don'ts. There was no love or mercy involved with being Jewish. If a Gentile chose to become a part of the family they had to go through certain cleansing processes. After they were accepted as a Gentile Jew, they could then take part in certain rituals and come into certain parts of the temple, God's house, but they were still treated as if the Jews were doing them a favor. They were never allowed to be 100% Jewish like a natural bloodline Jew.

If we take a close look at our concept of Christianity we can see the similarity. Do we not tell the sinners that it is their choice to become a Christian, as if a person can choose their Father? Do we not make them feel they are the scum of the earth and that they will go to hell if they don't change, but because it is the Christian thing to do we will tell them about Jesus, and invite them into the family "just as they are." Once an individual receives Jesus as their personal savior and has confessed they are a sinner we allow them into the church membership. From there we expect them to change and become a part of the dos and don'ts of the family of God so they can present a good "Christian" testimony for the ego of the church. If we were honest with ourselves we would see that this testimony is more for ourselves and the church than for the lost because they really don't care if we are keeping the commandments of legalism anyway. If anything, it gives them an excuse to show there is hypocrisy in the church. This is pretty much the pattern we see in Western Christianity of how the word "adoption" is used in Scripture.

In John 15:16 we read, *"Ye have not chosen me, but I have chosen you, and ordained you."* We cannot choose Jesus, for He has already chosen us. Ephesians 1:4 says, *"According as he hath chosen us in him before the foundation of the world."* The next response I usually encounter with these thoughts is, "Does this mean that God has already chosen who will go to heaven and who won't?" God is not a Father that picks and chooses which of His children He will keep and which He will let go to hell. He is all love, all powerful, and not afraid of anything, including any "evil" that may occur in our lives that we think could possibly separate us from His love. Those of us who think He could separate Himself from His children don't really know Him as Father God, but as a god of a religious system under the law of the old covenant.

The real implication of the word "adoption" which Scripture talks about is not that a family is taking in a stranger, but that a blood born child of the father has moved into maturity to do the father's business. Children were raised by a bondservant. This servant chose to be a part of this family, and his only responsibility was to teach the children to be a miniature duplication of their father. When the child became a certain age to where the father was able to see and hear himself there would be a great feast for the child. At this time the father would publicly present his son to let others know how well pleased he is with the character of this child. In the natural, the child was given a robe by a Roman father called a Toga Virila, and a Jewish father would give a Prayer Shawl or cloak with the family colors to the son. This took place with Jesus when John baptized him. The Father declared that this was his son in whom he was well pleased, and gave him the cloak of the family, the Holy Spirit. Before this ceremony Jesus was still the Son of God, but God saw him as a child, not ready to do the Father's business. This is also the coat of many colors that Joseph received from his father Jacob. His brothers were very angry with this because they knew the coat represented that Joseph was given the responsibility to oversee the family's business. This was normally the blessing given to the first born of the father.

These coverings declared that the father had given the son his blessing to represent him so that when others saw the son they saw the father. Romans 8 and Galatians 3 tell us of the Biblical concept of adoption. Also, in Galatians 4:1-2 we read, *"Now I say, that the heir as long as he is a child, differed nothing from a servant, though he be lord of all; but is under tutors and governors until the time appointed of the father."*

Many of us call ourselves Christians, but do we really walk as one? Biblically, children are Christians who need to be cared for. They don't give to others, but take care of their own needs to make sure they are getting to heaven to get all their inheritance. A child Christian can be a child for a long time. God does not give maturity to sons based on time. Many children of God are being faithful in going to church, being a part of the body of Christ, reading and meditating on the word of God, being prosperous, and seeing miracles. However, they are still children.

A son is one that has a heart that says when you see me, you see the Father. You see unconditional love, unconditional mercy, and unconditional forgiveness. The son does nothing except what he sees the Father do. A son says to himself that his purpose is not for others to see him, but to see the Father in him so that the Father will be glorified, and the children will be drawn to their Father.

We are at a great time of change and transformation. What we see in the natural is giving us insight into the spiritual. One of the major reasons that terrorists have had control is because of the disunity we have displayed in America in the church in regard to our understanding of Father God. Ask a Muslim who their god is and they will all share the same answer. Ask an American Christian who their God is and you will get their denomination's interpretation of what the Scriptures say about who God is. In America, we have the Methodist Father, the Baptist Father, the Lutheran Father, the

Catholic Father, etc. These brothers and sisters in Christ don't speak from the same understanding of what Father God is saying. Even though we all profess to be Christians, the diversity of doctrines brings diversity to the body of Christ. We worship and teach the same God and teach from the same bible, but American Christians have disunity in their concept of the character and nature of God. Christianity has become a religion instead of a relationship displaying the love and mercy of our Father.

Christianity today has not been practiced as a life of faith that matches the pattern our Heavenly Father created of parents having children. Instead we teach that it is the child who must choose their parent (spiritual father). We are practicing a form of religion where children are having children, one that reflects if you're a Christian then supposedly you have full understanding of what the Bible says, even though you don't, versus the mature Christians teaching the younger in love.

We have brought separation into the house of God by calling our brothers and sisters in Christ different names that don't belong to the family. When we recognized one another by the denomination of a church they attend versus the fact that we are a Christ One, we are name-calling. These names are not of our Father, but of our own creation. We use these names lifting them up higher than Scripture itself being a Baptist, Methodist, Lutheran, etc. The focus has shifted from exalting God as the Almighty One to recognizing a denomination having power in itself.

It is the Family of God that is supposed to be leading the way for transformation of the world, yet we bring disgrace to the Father with childish games. When others see us they should see the Father; our Father and their Father. Can people say that about you? Can people say that the love, mercy, and forgiveness of the Father flows out of you, and that your judgment is only of yourself?

The real battle of this world is not natural, but spiritual (Ephesians 6:12). We must be one people united under our Father God with His power and authority. We have the power of Life and Death in our tongues. We must stop using this power on others, and begin to cleanse our own house and see the finished work of Jesus Christ in others whether they see it or not, so that by His Love all men will be drawn to the family of our Heavenly Father.

3

Hear the Word of the Lord

In John, Chapter 11, as we read about the death of Lazarus we are being made aware of the reality of the way Martha and Mary believed concerning the death of their brother. His death reflected the limitations of their belief and relationship with the Messiah. The first command in Romans 10:17 is for us to "hear" what the Spirit of God is saying to us: *"So then faith cometh by hearing, and hearing by the word of God."* The Holy Spirit speaks to the Word seed in us and causes it to grow. God does not need natural ears to be heard. His voice is heard from the belly, not the head. *"Out of his belly shall flow rivers of living water"* (John 7:38).

In Mark 7:33 Jesus put his fingers in the man's ears and spit on the man's tongue. The literal understanding of this miracle makes it difficult to interpret because Jesus purposely closed his natural ears with the fingers of God. This represents the closing of the natural mind to rational comprehension. Next, Jesus spit on the man's tongue. For a Jew to spit on someone was the most disgraceful action one could do in showing hatred. Why would Jesus display such an action? The man needed new ears, a new tongue, and a new way of seeing things. The tongue holds the power of life and death. The spit Jesus gave was the inner water of God, the Word, with His

DNA to bring forth a new life. Romans 8:8 say, *"So then they that are in the flesh cannot please God."*

If we take this word "flesh" literally then we have a problem because then we are claiming to please God is with our bodies. We would have no hope of pleasing Him if we truly took the word flesh to represent our natural body. We would need to die a natural death to have any hope of pleasing God if we use this word literally. We might as well have the mindset that suicide is okay if we believe this way. Sounds like the concept of what a terrorist believes in pleasing Allah. According to Ezekiel 18:32, Scripture contradicts this belief: *"For I have no pleasure in the death of him that dieth, saith the Lord God: wherefore turn yourselves, and ye live."*

The word "flesh" is not referring to the physical body, but the mindset of natural man. Jesus redeemed man in the totality of body, soul, and spirit (not just our spirit, and then the rest will come later after the flesh becomes aged and decayed).

In the Old Testament, a relationship with God started in the outer court and "worked" through to the inner court. Only the high priest made it to the inner court where God resided. We know today that God's residence is the entire temple including all courts, and our body is His temple according to Scripture which says, *"Know ye not that ye are the temple of God, and that the spirit of God dwelleth in you?"* (I Corinthians 3:16). Jesus went into the inner court to bring the finished work out. What did the inner court speak of? It spoke that God is love, God is mercy, God is light, God is eternal, and in Him there is no condemnation. This is the voice that Jesus brought from the inner court to the activity of works in the middle and outer court. It is finished. We tend to focus on being like Jesus with the unconditional love and mercy, but put aside the fact that he was also an eternal being in the flesh.

Your body, soul, and spirit have been redeemed by the blood of Jesus! The corruptible must put on incorruptible. Let us read I Corinthians 15:50-58, *"Now this I say, brethren, that flesh and blood cannot inherit the kingdom of God; neither doth corruption inherit incorruption. Behold, I show you a mystery; we shall not all sleep, but we shall all be changed. In a moment, in the twinkling of an eye, at the last trump, for the trumpet shall sound, and the dead shall be raised incorruptible, and we shall be changed. For this corruptible must put on incorruption, and this mortal must put on immortality. So when this corruptible shall have put on incorruption, and this mortal shall be brought to pass the saying that is written, Death is swallowed up in victory. O death, where is thy sting? O grave, where is thy victory? The sting of death is sin, and the strength of sin is the law. But thanks be to God, which giveth us the victory through our Lord Jesus Christ. Therefore, my beloved brethren, be ye steadfast, unmovable, always abounding in the work of the Lord, for as much as ye know that your labor is not in vain in the Lord."*

Other Scriptures to consider are:

"For the law of the Spirit of life in Christ Jesus hath made me free from the law of sin and death." (Romans 8:2)

"And if Christ be in you, the body is dead because of sin; but the Spirit is life because of righteousness. But if the spirit of him that raised up Jesus from the dead dwell in you, he that raised up Christ from the dead shall also quicken your mortal bodies by his Spirit that dwelleth in you." (Romans 8:10-11)

"For if ye live after the flesh, ye shall die: but if ye through the Spirit do mortify the deeds of the body, ye shall live." (Romans 8:13) These Scriptures have been read and taught by many leaders of the church who speak of an end times, or rapture manifestation. They are also taught with a mindset of separation to describe mankind as saved or non-saved. I have put emphasis on the word "ALL" and "the dead shall be raised incorruptible" for you to take some thought in noticing that Paul did not say saved or non-saved. These Scriptures are telling us about life and death while in the natural body. True death is to be asleep while the Word is resident inside us. Mary and Martha were just as "asleep" as Lazarus was.

Paul shows us in Verses 44-49 of I Corinthians 15 the pattern of how God creates: *"It is sown a natural body; it is raised a spiritual body. There is a natural body, and there is a spiritual body. And so it is written, the first man Adam was made a living soul; the last Adam was made a quickening spirit. How be it that was not first which is spiritual, but that which is natural; and afterward that which is spiritual. The first man is of the earth, earthy: the second man is the Lord from heaven. As is the earthy, such are they also that are earthy: and as is the heavenly, such are they also that are heavenly. And as we have borne the image of the earthy, we shall also bear the image of the heavenly."* It is the same pattern found in Genesis, Chapters 1 and 2. First, He completes in the spirit realm. Next, He makes the earthly patterned after the finished spirit creation. Lastly, He brings the earthly into the heavenly so that He is All in All. The earthly brings tangibility to the heavenly. This is a good place to pause to think about the pattern of creation.

Let us continue with reading Verses 50-58 which reveals to us that the natural mind is not capable of inheriting the things of God or bringing earth and heaven together as one. *"Now this I say, brethren, that flesh and blood cannot inherit the kingdom of God; neither doth corruption inherit incorruption. Behold, I show you a mystery; We shall not all sleep, but we shall ALL be changed. In a moment, in the twinkling of an eye, at the last trump, for the trumpet shall sound, and the dead shall be raised incorruptible, and we shall be changed. For this corruptible must put on incorruption, and this mortal must put on immortality. So when this corruptible shall have put on incorruption, and the mortal shall have put on immortality, then shall be brought to pass the saying that is written, Death is swallowed up in victory. O death, where is thy sting? O grave, where is thy victory? The sting of death is sin; and the strength of sin is the law. But thanks be to God, which giveth us the victory through our Lord Jesus Christ. Therefore, my beloved brethren, be ye steadfast, unmovable, always abounding in the work of the Lord, for as much as ye know that your labor is not in vain in the Lord."*

For the manifestation of the inheritance that is ours now, let us look at Verse 53 again: *"For the corruptible must put on incorruption, and this mortal must put on immortality."* A spirit is not corruptible or mortal. The corruptible/mortal part is referring to the body and soul of man. When we allow the Holy Spirit in us to release the power that raised Jesus from the grave we move to Verses 54-58.

Let's back up to Verses 51-52 first. *"Behold I show you a mystery; we shall not all sleep, but we shall all be changed. In a moment, in the twinkling of an eye, at the last trump, for the trumpet shall sound, and the dead shall be raised incorruptible, and we shall be changed."* As you read these verses let's ponder a few of the words. The word "mystery" is sharing the fact that the knowledge was not known before, but is now revealed by the Holy Spirit available to be received in the present.

We shall not all sleep…sleep is to die with the seed of God inside you, but not utilizing the power of the Holy Spirit to overcome death, hell, and the grave. Jesus had the keys to these in which he took all judgment and condemnation. Revelation 1:18 says, *"I am he that liveth, and was dead; and, behold, I am alive forevermore, Amen; and have the keys of hell and of death."* This is why the second part of the verse says we shall all be changed. This is the manifestation that will occur because Jesus died for all mankind (he took away the sins of the world). Hebrews 2:9 tells us, *"But we see Jesus, who was made a little lower than the angels for the suffering of death, crowned with glory and honor that he by the grace of God should taste death for every man."*

Verse 52 also talks of the twinkling of an eye at the last trump. The word of God brings transformation. It happens faster than blinking your eye. Each of us has a last trump. The grand finale of corruptible becoming incorruptible will be when the Holy Spirit has pulled the veil revealing our true identity to be manifested as the sons of God in our natural body. It is up to us to walk in that inheritance by putting on incorruption each time we have a choice to bless or judge another. A choice of whether or not to release our God identity to someone that doesn't deserve it with unconditional love, mercy, and forgiveness. Each time we do this, we are clothing the corruptible with incorruption and the mortal with immortality.

Verse 54 comes with glory to the Father, *"death is swallowed up in victory."* It is not the will of God for us to go through death of the body in order for us to have a victorious relationship with Him in body, soul, and spirit. Jesus already took the penalty of sin for us and overcame death. The work is finished. It is up to us to see it brought forth by faith that the Word of God is truth and life whether our natural eyes see it or not. If our generation doesn't bring forth the finished work of Jesus Christ then God will simply use the next or the next. Time is not an issue with God.

Our Heavenly Father is not afraid of death. Jesus did away with it. In John 12:31-32 we read, *"Now is the judgment of this world: now shall the prince of this world be cast out. And I, if I be lifted up from the earth, will draw all men unto me."* Jesus was lifted up over two thousand years ago. We are to look at the life of others as the life of God in each individual giving no place to death. In order for the Lord of lords to return bringing heaven and earth together there must be a company of people who know they are the sons of God, for all of creation is groaning for them to be manifested (Romans 8:22). It will be the sons of God who transform the earth. A people that manifest God's faith will be transformed and not die a natural death. It will take the mind of Christ to manifest the inheritance the Father has given to His children. The mind of Christ is the reality that today, or NOW, is ALL that really exists. The past is gone and tomorrow is not here. When we focus on the issue of yesterday or tomorrow, we give place to a false reality that may seem good, but it is one that robs us of the peace that surpasses our understanding in Christ Jesus.

"Blessed are the peacemakers: for they shall be called the children of God." (Matthew 5:9)

"For as many as are led by the spirit of God, they are the Sons of God." (Romans 8:14)

4

Heaven is the Substance of Reality

"For whom he did foreknow, he also did predestinate to be conformed to the image of his son, that he might be the firstborn among many brethren." (Romans 8:29)

When God created man he gave him His nature and name so that everything in heaven would have a natural counterpart in the earth manifested in a form. To manifest the Sons of God we must experience God, which is Spirit, in the form of our natural body.

Jesus had to die two thousand years ago to bring visibility to the natural counterpart of what is in the heavens. In the natural, the counterpart of light is a shadow. In the heavens there is no shadow. Jesus had to overcome the natural, governed by time, to do away with time while on the earth. *"The earth is the Lord's, and the fullness thereof; the world, and they that dwell therein"* (Psalms 24:1). He came to take back what was his. Psalm 119:64 says, *"The earth, O Lord, is full of thy mercy: teach me thy statutes."* In Isaiah 11:9 we read, *"They shall not hurt nor destroy in ALL my holy mountain: for the earth shall be full of the knowledge of the Lord, as the waters cover the sea."*

The earth as we have known it is a counterpart of the truth which is heaven. Heaven is also here now because of what Jesus did. We just haven't recognized this. When we look at the counterpart, instead of the truth in the Word, we limit ourselves in time. However, when we realize that what we see is a shadow of reality, then we seek reality (truth, heaven), and bring it into the natural. Light always overcomes darkness or shadows.

Heaven is the substance of reality just as faith is the substance of things hoped for (Hebrews 11:1). It is the place of the embodiment of God: absolute, eternal, one, pure, light, life, love, mercy…

The earth is an appearance. Everything we see, hear, smell, taste, etc. with our senses in the natural is temporal. Everything in the natural is a shadow. Death is a shadow of Life. Psalms 23:4 says, *"Yea, though I walk through the valley of the shadow of death…"*

The substance of tangible things is in the Spirit (Hebrews 11:1). You can't see unconditional love and forgiveness because it is Spirit. You see the shadow that has touched the soul of man's natural senses with the manifestation of the Spirit by revelation and mercy. The Garden of Eden is a spiritual place where heaven and earth come together. All mankind has heaven and earth within them, but one must be a believer in the faith of Christ for the manifestation of heaven to come forth on earth. *"Be ye therefore followers of God as dear children: and walk in love, as Christ also hath loved us, and hath given himself for us as an offering and a sacrifice to God for a sweet smelling savor"* (Ephesians 5:1-2). *"For ye were sometimes darkness, but now are ye light in the Lord: walk as children of light"* (Ephesians 5:8).

The difference between a believer and a nonbeliever is that a believer knows that while he was yet dead in sin Jesus Christ took his sin, forgave, and cleansed him from all his unrighteousness. A nonbeliever doesn't know that they are already forgiven. Even before a believer knows the truth, the blood of Jesus has already cleansed them at Calvary two thousand years ago. Then when they come to know the Father's love by the drawing of the Holy Spirit they receive the good news and hope of what the blood of Jesus has ALREADY completed in heaven to bring this reality into their time.

Consider this illustration: There once were two male children born to a family. The first child was kidnapped at birth, and raised by another family that told him he was bad and evil. This is all this child knew about himself until one day he found out that these people were not his real parents. When he becomes an adult he goes in search of his real father, which brings him to a huge country estate. He goes through the front gate and as he travels the road to the house he is stopped by a man. After talking with the man they are both made aware that they are brothers. The second man is eager to take his brother to their father's house. As they make a turn in the road they see a huge castle. The second son opens the door where their father is waiting, for the father had seen both men coming down the road and recognized that both boys belonged to him. However, when the first son comes to the door he does not consider himself worthy enough to take part in his father's home, and he insists in staying in the stables. He's willing to live on the estate, but only as a servant and not as a son.

The ministry of Christians is to reconcile nonbelievers to our Father, and their Father, by the Holy Spirit in us, that we may be one with God. To do this we must already see the nonbeliever as a child of God. Instead, we have traditionally displayed a spirit of segregation and self-centeredness. For example, a pattern displayed by many Christians is, "I'm saved, and you're not. I'm going to Heaven, you're going to Hell."

What we must realize is that ALL mankind is the body of Christ. For the fullness of the body to come forth we must as Sons of God declare the peace and righteousness of the inheritance to ALL mankind. We must intercede for nonbelievers so the Holy Spirit will draw them to our Father just as Jesus did for those that believe.

Every time we accept in our heart that a nonbeliever has gone to Hell, we must hold ourselves accountable for sending them there versus having faith in the intercession which allows us to claim them as our household, as stated in Acts 16:31, *"Believe on the Lord Jesus Christ, and thou shalt be saved, and thy house."*

God has given us the example in the natural of how we are created to understand the usage of the word "body" in Scripture. When a new life is being created in a mother's womb all of the parts of that creation are formed before the baby leaves the mother. At the time of the birth the baby has all the toes and fingers and other body parts that will forever belong to his body. The baby will not have an arm "grafted in" later that can become part of his body because there will be no blood. However, the body will go through stages of development to manifest all of what was originally created at birth in the DNA, but not yet revealed.

This is how we need to see mankind. To say that a nonbeliever has been grafted into the body of Christ because they have been drawn by the Holy Spirit to the Father and now believes in Jesus Christ as their personal savior leaves an opportunity for scars to develop that don't heal. They become barriers to receiving the fullness of the body's blood and immune system. It also leaves open the opportunity for the body to reject the part that was "grafted in." The interpretation of adoption and "grafted in" approach taught by tradition may appear to make sense according to Western theology in order to become part of the family of God, but it goes against God's character, nature, and design of creation. It leaves room for imperfection making a place for the enemy. God does not share His body, His house, with anyone. As discussed in Chapter 2, we must look into the Biblical cultural to understand what was meant with the words "adoption" and "grafted in" by the author.

Our children belong to us because of our bloodline as the parents. Whether or not they are raised by us, and whether or not they accept us as parents cannot alter the bloodline. We are children of God by the blood of Jesus that was shed two thousand years ago. The genealogy of Jesus to Adam, and Adam to Jesus found in Genesis 5 and Luke 3 tells us that the entire genealogy of mankind is the bloodline of God calling ALL mankind as the sons of God.

The household or body represents more than just a natural family linage. It represents every cell of the body of Christ. Christ Jesus came to fulfill the will of our Father, which is that none shall perish. *"The Lord is not slack concerning his promise as some men count slackness: but is longsuffering to us-ward, not willing that any should perish, but that all should come to repentance"* (2 Peter 3:9). Jesus fulfilled this by shedding his own blood for the sins of the world. He is the head, and we are the body. It is His Spirit that speaks to the woman (natural man, or soul of man) to bring forth the fullness of the bride of Christ (all mankind) without spot or wrinkle.

If it were possible for one person to be lost the way Christianity is taught today then Satan would be able to defeat God, and we could never expect the return of Jesus Christ because His bride would never be brought to completion without spot or wrinkle. We would be lost forever, and the cross would not have accomplished the will of the Father that none should perish (John 6:36-38).

If our hearts truly hunger and thirst for the return of our Lord Jesus Christ, we must begin with the Garden of Eden that we have within us. We have power and authority to forgive sins and to set the captives free. We are to "be fruitful, and multiply," and "replenish the earth, and subdue it" (Gen. 1:28).

The seed of God has been planted into the womb (heart) of every person before the foundations of the world; *"Before I formed thee in the belly I knew thee; and before thou camest forth out of the womb I sanctified thee, and ordained thee a prophet unto the nations"* (Jeremiah 1:5). It is up to us to bring forth the Word, the water, that nonbelievers may hear, and by hearing; the seed within them will grow. *"Faith comes by hearing, and hearing by the word of God"* (Romans 10:17). The seed will be hindered in growth if there is judgment and condemnation, *"for law is not of faith"* (Galatians 3:12). Judgment and condemnation are the weeds of the world. Growth comes from the manifestation of the unconditional love and forgiveness of the Father brought forth by the Holy Spirit manifested in the sons of God. Galatians 2:20 tells us, *"I live by the faith of the Son of God."*

God is not limited by time. If this generation doesn't grow up to do the Father's will, then God will go to the next. In Matthew 25:31-46 we read about the Son of man coming in his glory (his bride, the Sons of God) to separate the sheep from the goats. Both of these animals have significance in explaining the order of growth and development that we go through in bringing forth the kingdom of God. Let's take a look at this parable in Matthew 25 to get a better understand of what is being spoken.

"When the Son of man shall come in his glory, and all the holy angels with him, then shall he sit upon the throne of his glory and before him shall be gathered all nations: and he shall separate them one from another, as a shepherd divideth his sheep from the goats: and he shall set the sheep on his right hand, but the goats on the left. Then shall the King say unto them on his right hand, Come, ye blessed of my Father, inherit the kingdom prepared for you from the foundation of the world: for I was hungry and ye gave me meat: I was thirsty, and ye gave me drink: I was a stranger, and ye took me in: naked, and ye clothed me: I was sick, and ye visited me: I was in prison, and ye came unto me. Then

shall the righteous answer him, saying, Lord, when saw we thee hungry, and fed thee? Or thirsty, and gave thee drink? When saw we thee a stranger and took thee in? Or naked, and clothed thee? Or when saw we thee sick, or in prison, and came unto thee? And the King shall answer and say unto them, Verily I say unto you, in as much as ye have done it unto one of the least of these my brethren; ye have done it unto me. Then shall he say also unto them on the left hand, depart from me, ye cursed, unto everlasting fire, prepared for the devil and his angels: for I was hungry and ye gave me no meat: I was thirsty, and ye gave me no drink: I was a stranger, and ye took me not in naked, and ye clothed me not: sick, and in prison, and ye visited me not. Then shall they also answer him saying, Lord, when saw we thee hungry, or a thirst, or a stranger, or naked, or sick, or in prison, and did not minister unto thee? Then shall he answer them, saying, Verily I say unto you, inasmuch as ye did it not to one of the least of these, ye did it not to me. And these shall go away into everlasting punishment, but the righteous into life eternal."

This passage of Scripture is not found in any of the other gospels, so we must go to other areas of the Bible to get a better understanding of what Matthew was talking about. Tradition teaches that these Scriptures are referring to a future judgment of separation between the believers, called sheep, and the nonbelievers, called goats. The believers are sitting at the Son of man's right hand (Jesus/God) and will go to heaven. The nonbelievers are sitting at His left hand and will be going to hell. When the Lord talks about feeding the hungry and clothing the naked, there is more to understand beyond the natural picture of giving food and clothes.

First of all, we stated earlier that God is not limited to time, so to read these Scriptures as a point of time in the future goes against God's character, nature, and His word in John 5:22 that tell us He will not be judging any man. If we research the difference between goats and sheep used in this parable we find they are of the same family. They were both considered clean animals so both were used for food, clothing, and sin offerings. The unique difference between them is that the goats have a character of independence (self-centered) and the sheep are very dependant upon the shepherd's care. Either one could be used to illustrate a child of God. With these thoughts in mind, let us turn to Proverbs 3:11-12, *"My son* (goat or sheep)*, despise not the chastening of the Lord; neither be weary of his correction: For whom the Lord loveth he correcteth; even as a father the son in whom he delighteth."* Can a parent that loves their child unconditionally send the child to hell? If we believe it is possible then we nullify the unconditional love of the Father who sent his son Jesus to take upon himself the sins of the world.

In Matthew 25, we read about the right hand and left hand of the King, which we know to be Jesus, the King of kings. It doesn't make sense to think that the hand of God is heaven on the right and hell on the left, yet this is the theology concept that most churches teach. In Proverbs 3:13 we read, *"Happy is the man that findeth wisdom, and the man that getteth understanding."* In Isaiah Chapter 11, Verse 2, we are told that wisdom and understanding are part of the spirit of the Lord. *"And the spirit of the Lord shall rest upon him, the spirit of wisdom and understanding, the spirit of counsel and might, the spirit of knowledge and of the fear of the Lord."* Proverbs 3:16 says, *"Length of days is in her* (Spirit of the Lord*) right hand; and in her left hand* *riches and honor."* How can God's word be positive to sit at His left hand in Proverbs, but be interpreted as negative in Matthew 25? How can God who is Love, Light, Life, and Eternal with no darkness have a "good side" to sit on and a supposedly "bad side"?

If we continue reading from Proverbs 3:18, *"She (wisdom/understanding) is a tree of life to them that lay hold upon her: and happy is everyone that retaineth her. The Lord by wisdom hath founded the earth; by understanding hath he established the heavens."* God's left hand balances out the right hand, but both hands are the Tree of Life.

When reading this parable in a literal sense it sounds like the word "eternal" or "everlasting" is connected with a positive and negative connotation sending people to Heaven or Hell depending on works. God is His word, and the word Eternal is God. Nothing else exists eternally except God. Eternally, God is All in All (Ephesians 4:6). The word Life is God, and the word Fire is God for He is a consuming fire. Any negative connotations of doom and gloom for the goats must be reconsidered to line up with the witness of other Scriptures.

We have been given a type and shadow for the place of God's residence, which was first given to Moses to create after a heavenly pattern given by God in the Old Testament. His temple in the New Testament is our bodies which we previously discussed and is made up of three courts as patterned in the Old Testament. Those that are using God's word in an unconditional way to show mercy, love, and forgiveness to others so that His character is being seen are the sheep that are clothing and feeding the spiritually needy. They have experienced the eternal blessing of life found in the inner court of God's temple, known as the Holy of Holies, and bring His love to the rest of His body in the middle, or Holy place, and outer courts.

Those that use the word of God to bring law and judgment to others are the goats. Their understanding of a relationship with the Father is locked into their hearts of being a sinner, repentance, and works trying to kill the flesh found in the outer court. When they see others sinning they use the word of God to bring judgment and condemnation against them thinking they can beat goodness into them by justification. The middle and inner courts are protected from heat, rain, snow, drought, etc. However, the outer court is continuously being exposed to the elements of nature, or the world issues. In the inner and middle courts there is no time or season. Many Christians nullify the cross bringing grievance to the Holy Spirit that the finished work of Jesus Christ isn't quite enough, because they choose to stay in the outer court seeing life with natural eyes versus the spiritual eyes of God. We are told not to grieve the Holy Spirit (Ephesians 4:30). What else is there for Jesus to do that wasn't accomplished at his resurrection and ascension? This is why Christians who think they are sheep may really be goats who are waiting for the finished work to come forth, never receiving the fullness of their inheritance that is available to them today.

The manifested sons of God will always see restoration, wholeness, completeness, and the finished work of Heaven NOW in the midst of time. It is the love of God energized by the intimacy with God in the inner court, which brings forth the faith that overcomes death, hell, and the grave. God came to this earth as the Son of man to show us how man is to function as His children or gods.

Ezekiel 37:12 says, *"Therefore prophesy and say unto them, Thus saith the Lord God: Behold, my people, I will open your graves* (judgment/the natural mind's creation), *and bring you into the land of Israel."* Can we dare to think that what our natural minds have been taught that we are sinners as an identity is greater than what God says of who we are as a Son of God created in His image?

God chose to die through Jesus so that ALL men would be free from the death penalty. Everything is done by the faith of God, not our faith, but His faith in us by the Holy Spirit. We are to rise up by His faith with a conviction of Knowing that God has already completed before He began, and that He is ALL in ALL NOW. The more law, literal concepts, and natural understandings of the interpretation of the things of God, the less faith is required. However, the less faith a person has in their relationship with God versus the need to "see it" to "believe it," the more separated a person will be from God.

"But God hath chosen the foolish things of the world to confound the wise; and God hath chosen the weak things of the world to confound the things which are might." (I Corinthians 1:27)

Going back to the sheep and goats, Matthew 26 shows that the chief priest and scribes knew what Jesus was talking about in regard to the sheep and goat mentality and tried to kill him. They had a responsibility to be "sheep" to the people of God, and instead they took on a "goat" mentality using God's word to lift them up and to bring judgment and condemnation to His children. Yes, the scribes and Pharisees were part of God's family, but they were so consumed with their own self-righteousness that they didn't recognize "Love" when it stood next to them. All they saw was the son of a carpenter. How often do we see others from the outer court mindset versus the heart of the Father?

Jeremiah 3:15 says, *"I will give you pastors according to mine heart, which shall feed you with knowledge and understanding."* Isaiah 61:10 tells us, *"He hath clothed me with the garments of salvation, he hath covered me with the robe of righteousness, as a bridegroom decketh himself with ornaments, and as a bride adorneth herself with her jewels."*

When we go before the Lord as an intercessor we are to feed, encourage, edify, and lift up the nonbeliever with the Word, and clothe them with righteousness, unconditional love, mercy, and forgiveness. They are clean whether they receive it or not as far as the Father is concerned. When we come before the Father, he will judge if we interceded for others as Jesus did for us, or if we judged others sending nonbelievers to hell with our thoughts and words. Jesus has the keys of death and of hell (Revelation 1:18). If we did send them there we have the ability to bring them back by the power and authority as the Sons of God based on the fact that He is the head and we are His body.

Let it be said by our bridegroom, *"Verily I say unto you, inasmuch as ye have done it unto one of the least of these my brethren, ye have done it unto me."* (Matt. 25:40)

5

Do We Have Two Minds?

"And seek not ye what ye shall eat, or what ye shall drink, neither be ye of doubtful mind." Luke 12:28

"A double minded man is unstable in all his ways." James 1:8

Power and authority of the Christian life cannot flow through a mixture, or double mind. Everything going on in the mind of Christ is complete and set in motion. Jesus spent 30 years learning and growing before He went out to deal with mixed minds. He had to be trained to grow from being a child of God to a Son of God. When he got the approval of the Father, *"Thou art my beloved Son; in thee I am well pleased"* (Luke 33:22), Jesus received the authority of the Father to do the Father's business, but because his greatest confrontation came from the religious system, he was not able to do great works in the temples. He had to go into the highways and byways for miracles to be seen.

Whatever you surround yourself with is what you will bring into your life and mindset. Let's think of the Scriptures that talk about two men and two women found in Luke 17:31-37. These Scriptures are usually referred to with a pretribulation or rapture accordance. Verse 34 has many times been used to refer to homosexual activity, yet we don't take into account that this is God speaking with unconditional love, mercy, and forgiveness. The two men in the one bed is God showing one man with a double mind (the mind of the first Adam and the mind of Jesus). The first Adam must go, and the mind of Jesus Christ will stay. The same can be applied to the next verses about the two women and the two men in the field. Verse 37 tells us that the body of Christ will be as eagles, reaching high and seeing as the Father sees past what is in the natural.

Have you ever noticed that many times the body of Christ will treat people differently depending on the issue involved? We will pray for people, love and surround them with compassion if they are dealing with cancer, diabetes, or heart attacks. However, we tend to express a different mindset toward those caught in adultery or homosexuality. We may forgive them because we know we are supposed to, but our hearts still contain judgment and condemnation. Cancer, diabetes, and heart disease are usually connected with poor lifestyle choices, yet we are more compassionate to people with these problems, even if they were caused from drinking or smoking. What about the health-care person that gets a blood disease from a patient, but is also having an affair and contracts a sexually transmitted disease? Should we treat people with compassion when they are victims, but then with judgment when they acquire a life threatening disease doing something they shouldn't have been doing? As Christians, how is the mind of Christ being seen?

In Acts Chapter 10, Peter struggled with a mixed mindset, as we do today. Jesus saw ALL mankind as cleansed by the blood that he shed for the sins of the world (John 1:29). He knew the fullness of that cleansing before the cross, which is why miracles took place before Calvary. He saw people as whole and complete (body, soul, and spirit) BEFORE He rose from the grave. The finished work was already done before the foundations of the world (I Peter 1:20). Jesus came to set the captives free from the bondages they were in by manifesting that which was already completed (Luke 4:18).

There is a calendar available of firemen that served in the rescuing of the September 11, 2001 attack against the United States. These firemen represent the multitude of people that gave their lives for strangers. Looking at the calendar you may see the physical attractiveness of these men, or you may see the self-less sacrifice of their lives for others. Should we ask what was going on in their personal life? Should we ask what was going on in the personal lives of the people they were trying to save? Statistics will show that you could probably find every sin imaginable within the number of people involved in this traumatic event in history (those who were seeking to be rescued, those who were doing the rescuing, and those who died).

However, was anyone making a deciding factor of who to help or not help depending on if they were having an affair, cheating on their spouse, doing drugs, or living a life of homosexuality, etc? Those firemen and officers represented the heart of what Christianity is supposed to portray everyday by giving our lives to a stranger. Ask yourself how many strangers have come across your path that you interceded in prayer for asking God to bless them whether they asked for it or not, or whether they were nice to you or not? Do you put your life down to allow the life of the Lord Jesus in you to shine through you? We have wasted so much time picking and choosing between what is and what is not God that we as Christians are not manifesting the fullness of our inheritance that Jesus gave us in John 20.

What is real double mindedness? We struggle with this today because Christianity teaches us that a life with Christ is "a little bit now, but hang on and you'll get the rest when you get to heaven." Religion says you'll get the fullness of Christ after your body dies. This concept sounds good because we see the aging process as our bodies are in bondage with time until time has brought death.

However, the Bible gives us witnesses in both Old and New Testaments of incidents where the flesh overcame death while in the body. Some examples of this can be found in: 2 Kings 2 with Elijah, Genesis 5:24 with Enoch, Matt. 9 with Jairus' daughter, Luke 7 with the widow's son, John 7 with Lazarus, Acts 9 with Dorcas raised by Peter, and in Matthew 27:52 where the graves were opened and the bodies of the Saints came out and entered the Holy City. If we really believe that God is the same yesterday, today, and forever as Hebrew 13:8 tells us, and if we also believe that God is no respecter of persons (Acts 10:34), then do we believe that God is big enough to bring His eternal presence into time today to do away with time? Have we been accepting less than what is available to us because we have been placing more emphasis on what our bodies and our senses speak to us versus the mind of Christ that is in us?

Hebrews 6 tells us to move beyond salvation, healing, and raising the dead. Do we even consider that our Heavenly Father has an inheritance that takes us beyond raising the dead? This salvation, healing, and raising the dead is not written for a personal, self-need in knowing there is life after death. God does not need to be taught how to have healing, prosperity, or wholeness manifested in His body. Sons of God would have the maturity to BE and do as their Father reveals for His glory to be seen. These are commissions that believers are required to intercede by faith to those who don't believe the gospel of hope; that there is hope in life beyond what their body and senses are telling them while in their flesh.

Did you ever think about the fact that you can't give away something that you don't have? It is a natural law that applies to everything. Let us challenge ourselves:

Do I believe in salvation, eternal life with Jesus Christ because of the cross and resurrection reuniting me as a child of God? Yes, I do. Now I can give that hope to someone else. Let's move on...the doctor says I have cancer of_____. God says I will heal you of ALL your wounds and ALL your afflictions (Jeremiah 30:17). I received my healing because I believe that I am my Father's child and that He is no respecter of persons. I believe that if my dad said it then it is done, and I will rest in His presence of when and how He wants the healing manifested so that He will be glorified. By faith, I know that I will either receive my healing on this side of life or on the other side, but it would be a greater testimony to the Father for me to be able to have the ability to tell others if I receive it on this side while in my earthly body. The healing comes and I now have something to give away to someone else who has been diagnosed with the same.

We should be able to see the same process with the resurrection of the dead. I know this is strong, but Jesus showed us the way. The power of the Holy Spirit raised Him up from the dead, and we should rest in the assurance of being raised up also. Acts 24:15 says, *"Have hope toward God, which they themselves also allow, that there shall be a resurrection of the dead, both of the just and unjust."* Just as Jesus glorified the Father by the finished work, He, being the head of our body, should have manifestation of glorifying the Father with our bodies overcoming death. Not for us to be invincible, but to declare that God is all in all. Philippians 3:10-11, *"That I may know him, and the power of his resurrection, and the fellowship of his sufferings, being made conformable unto his death; if by any means I might attain unto the resurrection of the dead."*

Transformation begins with salvation, by hearing the Word, and receiving the Word. Acceptance of a person's salvation is acknowledged by faith. There is no outward manifestation expected. It is a total work of faith within yourself whether anyone else sees it or not. There is no accountability other than what church doctrines have required from the testimony of their congregation to establish their own belief, but not necessarily the doctrine of God. Salvation is a stepping-stone in the relationship of being a child of God, but just as in the natural, there must be a growing up in spiritual maturity to hold ourselves accountable to do the Father's work. As we hear the word of our Father and believe, we must allow the fruit of the Holy Spirit in us to grow and develop. It is important that as a cell of the body of Christ we stay connected with the body and function as a corporate people in the love of the Father.

The signs, wonders, and miracles that Jesus did are not being seen by the children of God because we have not been walking in our true identity. It takes a son to walk with the authority of the Father in order for miracles to take place. Most Christians are scared of the "what if" versus the walking by faith in the Word. Can we really declare healing according to the Word of God and the power and authority given to us as a Son of God, yet not see the manifestation? We should be able to, but when we rely on our senses and emotions more than our faith, we don't.

A child will take what he needs for his own survival and pleasure. When we see our own children show compassion and unconditional love to others, we are moved with an unspeakable love for our children because of their maturity and growth beyond their needs. Throughout Scripture, the Bible speaks of children of God and sons of God. In the Old Testament there were those who knew they were children of God, and those called Gentiles who didn't know they were children of God. Both Jew and Gentile children were self-centered versus God-centered. There were those who were like the prodigal son (Gentiles), and those who thought they were better than everyone else (Jews), like the son that stayed home in the parable Jesus told in Luke 15. Neither son in this parable truly showed the maturity needed to do the Father's business, as a son should. They both manifested self-centered natures.

How do we fulfill the Scripture of John 14:12 that tell us we will do greater works than those that Jesus did? We must move beyond the double minded mentality of the Gentiles, Jews, and what we reflect as Christianity today. Christians must move into the mind of Christ (single-minded) as the Sons of God on the earth today to bring forth the manifestation of glory and honor to the Father.

Mark 12:29-31 reads, *"The first of all the commandments is Hear, O Israel: The Lord our God is one Lord: And thou shalt love the Lord thy God with all thy heart, and with all thy soul, and with all thy mind, and with all thy strength: this is the first commandment. And the second is like, namely this, Thou shalt love thy neighbor as thyself, there is none other commandment greater than these."*

These verses should challenge our understanding to receive the revelation that Christ is ALL in ALL, and in ALL (Colossians 3:11).

6

God's Habitation in You

"All things were made by him; and without him was not any thing made that was made." John 1:3

Think about these thoughts: God never inhabits anything that He has not built or created, and God always starts with a finished work. He is not within a mixture or amalgamation. God is within Himself; your body, soul, and spirit are His dwelling place.

When Moses was first given instructions to build a dwelling place for God he was instructed to start with the Holy of Holies. In Jeremiah 1:5, we are told that God already knew us before the foundations of the world, before we entered into our mother's womb. Now, with those thoughts, let's go to Scripture:

Exodus 20:3-5 says, *"Thou shall have no other gods before me. Thou shall not make unto thee any graven image or any likeness of any thing that is in heaven above, or that is in the earth beneath, or that is in the water under the earth. Thou shall not bow down thyself to them, nor serve them..."*

(A rabbit trail to go on is that this Scripture tells us that water, which represents the Word, is found under the earth (so much for where hell is supposed to be).

While Moses was up on the mountain, the children of God were making an image of a golden calf according to the way they saw God. In Exodus 32, Moses tried to go before the Lord to bring atonement for their sin. He went before God and declared that the people "had sinned a great sin" by making gods of gold. This is a picture of a people who were worshipping the wealth they possessed, (the root of all evil according to I Timothy 6:10). However, in Verse 32, Moses asked the Lord for their forgiveness, sacrificing his own life for their sake. God responds to Moses in the next verses by showing him the finished work of Jesus. It wouldn't be Moses that would blot out the sins of the people, although he knew the Son of God had the power to do this from his upbringing as Pharaoh's son. God told him to take the people to a place that He would visit and he sent the Angel of the Lord before them. This place was Calvary where all the sin of mankind has been atoned for by the blood of Jesus Christ. *"He was the lamb slain from the foundation of the world"* (Revelation 13:8). This took place in the spirit realm before creation in Genesis, Chapter 1 and 2. He became the Book of Life taking on flesh to do away with sin bringing in a New Covenant. Jesus existed in the very beginning before he was known as Jesus. We were ALL spiritually alive before we came into our bodies (Jeremiah 1:5), just as Jesus was the Angel of the Lord that came before us (Exodus 32:34).

God designed the Levitical Priesthood to be a representation (shadow) of what Jesus would manifest as the intercessor for all mankind. The feast days in the Old Testament were a celebration of a day that would come when sin would not be covered up, but done away with. Since no man was able to do away with sin, the tabernacle could not be built from the inside out as originally shown to Moses (Exodus 35), but had to be built from the outside in. The New Covenant is for the building of the tabernacle from the inside out (starting with the Holy of Holies and building to the outer court). However, what we call Christianity is still building from the outside in with a mindset of "get your foot in the door, get yourself born again." Then someday when you die, or if the "rapture" comes you can get into the Holy of Holies where God is. This is an example of outer court mentality.

According to Scripture, we had permission to go into the Holy of Holies two thousand years ago when Jesus was resurrected from the dead. *"Let us therefore come boldly unto the throne of grace that we may obtain mercy, and find grace to help in time of need"* (Heb. 4:16). In John 12:31-32 we are told, *"Now is the judgment of this world: now shall the prince of this world be cast out. And if I be lifted up from the earth, will draw all men unto me."* The NOW occurred at Calvary.

Moses was told to call Bezaleel from the tribe of Judah (Ex. 35:30) to build the tabernacle from the outside in. Our pastors and teachers today are still teaching the New Covenant from a Bezaleel mindset versus the finished work of Jesus Christ. Bezaleel had an Old Testament mindset which included rituals, regulations, formalities of doctrine that declared do's and don'ts, (what you eat, what you wear, who you hang around with, etc.) to justify the atonement for sin. It was about what man was capable of accomplishing for the cleansing of his sins based on works. We say we are saved by grace, yet we immediately plunge into rituals of formality to give a "good testimony" for the sake of being known as a Christian. We place others in bondage by judging them according to the standards we see in our doctrinal teachings versus judging as Jesus did from the mercy seat of God, the Holy of Holies.

Most Christians today live as if the New Covenant doesn't exist. The veil into the Holy of Holies was torn so we could go in, not so God could come out. We were meant to be the flesh that comes out from the presence of God to be the reality of who He is. We should be seen as High Priests, sons of God walking and talking as our Father with the mercy seat in us. *"And behold, the veil of the temple was rent in twain from top to the bottom"* (heaven was brought to earth), *and the earth did quake, and the rocks rent; and the graves were opened..."* (Matt. 27:51-52). All of creation was affected when the veil was rent bringing heaven to the earth, under the earth, and to the graves of death. The circle of life was brought into full manifestation with Jesus declaring in Revelation 1:17-18, *"Fear not; I am the first and the last: I am he that liveth, and was dead; and, behold, I am alive forevermore, Amen; and have the keys of hell and of death."* As Christians we should be rejoicing with the revelation to the world saying, *"O death, where is thy sting? O grave, where is they victory?"* (I Corinthians 15:55). *"But we see Jesus, who was made a little lower than the angels for the suffering of death, crowned with glory and honor; that he by the grace of God should taste death FOR EVERY MAN"* (Hebrews 2:9).

Let's think about a home and those that live in the home. Almost every society has the cultural basis of a man and woman being married first, and then having children. Anything other than this pattern does not give a clear picture of family structure in regards to the children. Religion accepts this pattern emphasizing that marriage comes first, and then children. This is the pattern established by God for the sanctification of the home in the natural world. Yet, is that same pattern taught for the sanctification of God's home, His kingdom?

Most denominations teach you to go out and bring people to Jesus Christ, winning souls for the kingdom of God. It is taught that we should bring people to accept Jesus as their personal savior so they can be "born again" as a child of God. All of this sounds good, but when is the marriage? How about the marriage feast? How is the marriage to Jesus taking place if you are being born again, and how is the consecration of the marriage happening so that children of God can be produced? Most religions will tell you that you are in an "engaged" state. Do we consider having intimacy with our beloved in an engaged relationship as the acceptable way to produce children? I know that it happens, but as parents, aren't we relieved when the couple gets married, especially if the woman is already pregnant?

From the spiritual aspect of family relations, we are taught that children can choose their parents (being born again is our choice), and then we also teach that it's okay to have sex before marriage if children of God are produced. Do we really believe that God has a different pattern of family formation other than what He created for us in the natural?

What does all this have to do with the Holy of Holies? WE HAVE THE POWER TO CREATE. Those that are teaching the Word from the mind of man versus the mind of Christ are the ones who are bringing adultery into the Holy of Holies. Jesus Christ fulfilled all the laws of the Old Testament. There is nothing more that he can do for His bride whom he married two thousand years ago, which is ALL mankind. He died for the sins of the world for all men (John 1:29). We receive the intimacy of the Spirit of God that waters and nourishes the seed of God already in us when we acknowledge our own crucifixion as in Galatians 2:20. Paul says in Gal. 3:3 *"Are ye so foolish? Having begun in the Spirit, are ye now made perfect by the flesh."* God knew us before the beginning of time and He made us perfect (Jeremiah 1:5). The sin (action) brought into the kingdom of God by Adam also brought time, flesh, and death. God made a way to have victory over time and death while still in the flesh illustrated by Jesus and the Disciples.

Have you ever wondered why there is no record of any Disciples dying a natural death? They were either martyred or they just disappeared. Have you ever wondered what happened to Lazarus after he came out of the grave, or how about the many saints whose graves were opened in Matt. 27:50-52? These are questions most theologians will try to justify with an answer like, "Those things happened then, but not now," or "Those coming out of the grave had to be born again receiving Jesus Christ as their personal savior." Tell me, if God opened your grave and claimed you as His child would you argue that you're an unworthy sinner? Would you argue with God about your identity if He called you His child? If you walked with God in the flesh as the Disciples did, or died and God raised you from the grave, where else would there be for you to go? Did they go back to the grave because the work that God did the first time wasn't good enough? Most preachers today will tell you that those that God raised from the dead had to die again until the second coming of the Lord. The cross at Calvary didn't quite finish the job. This is a religious mindset as illustrated in John 19:31 which says, *"The Jews therefore, because it was the preparation, that the bodies should not remain upon the cross on the Sabbath day,* (for that Sabbath day was a high day), *besought Pilate that their legs might be broken and that they might be taken away."* The Jews knew the Scriptures in Exodus 12:46 which state that the sacrificial lamb's bones were not to be broken. In Psalms 22:14 they knew that if Jesus was for filling Scripture that it was okay for his bones to be out of joint, but not broken. The Scriptures that tormented them were with Ezekiel's prophecies in Chapter 37 that there could be life found in bones that were not broken according to the verses in this chapter. The Jews were also familiar with the Egyptian culture that believes if one bone was broken of a body, the spirit could not return to the body from the afterlife. The Jews were so filled with hate for Jesus that they didn't want to take any chances that he might return. They didn't really believe in the resurrection of the dead, but "just to make sure" it wasn't possible they wanted to claim the body of Jesus, which meant the possibility of the legs needing to be broken for a hasty death.

Jesus came and died for the world (for all mankind) once. He completed the job. We were all married to our beloved two thousand years ago. When we share the good news of who we are now to those who are lost from a relationship with God, it should be with love letting them know that it isn't something for them to do, but to receive. If they don't receive, it doesn't change the fact that they are still a child of God. They are just missing out on the inheritance that is available for them to receive now while in the flesh. The prodigal son was still the son whether he came back to the father or not (Luke 15).

The elder son that stayed with the father in Luke 15 was angry because of the way his brother spent his inheritance, and he did not appreciate the way his father restored the brother's position. Interestingly, the father doesn't even scold his son or make any conditions for his return. The father eagerly gives him the power and authority of being part of the family before the son gives repentance. The elder brother was with the father the whole time the younger brother was spending all of his inheritance wrongly. He stayed with the father, but he didn't learn the father's mindset. The elder brother saw things from a tree of the knowledge of good and evil, or a right and wrong mindset. He was in "the field" (Luke 15:25) where serpents like to stay. Verse 32 shows the father's mindset in seeing the lost as our brothers in Christ Jesus. Our responsibility to the family of God, as the wife of our beloved, is to seek the lost children and show them the love of their Heavenly Father. The inheritance they can now have is the kingdom of God, which is righteousness, peace, and joy in the Holy Ghost (Romans 14:17).

We must realize that our place as New Testament children of God began in the Holy of Holies (at the cross), and then came out to the middle and outer courts. To bring forth the sons of God we must first acknowledge our identity as the wife of Jesus Christ. We then must take care of the children of God and show them their Heavenly Father.

7

The Return of Christ

"Beloved, we are (even here now) *God's children; it is not yet disclosed* (made clear) *what we shall be* (hereafter), *but we know that when He comes and is manifested, we shall* (as God's children) *resemble and be like Him, for we shall see Him just as He* (really) *is"* (I John 3:2 Amplified).

Is the appearing of Jesus Christ a one-day thing in the future, or a continual process manifested as revelation of the Word comes forth in our life (John 1:1)? Is the appearing of Jesus Christ subject to time, or is eternity brought into time to be in this world but not of this world (John 8:23)? Many of us read the verse above (I John 3:2) with an understanding that "yes," someday the Lord will return, but I probably won't see all of Him until I die. We have the mentality that God needs to use death as a vessel for us to travel through to see all of Christ. The words "when he appears" can be understood as "when we resemble." Whenever we have a revelation from God he becomes more real to us. The characteristics of God become tangible to us and flow through us. This is when his appearing becomes a manifestation of heaven brought forth in the earth. God is in the business of reduction so that anything that is not Him must go. He takes us through the "fire" to be refined, not burned up. Covenant with God is He is everything, and He takes you into His covenant to become everything in Him. It is not an equal partnership of sharing; it is God all in all (I Corinthians 15:28). It is not God and I, but ALL God and only God. Selah.

1 John 3:5 (Amplified) says, *"You know that He appeared in visible form and became Man to take away* (upon Himself*) sins, and in Him there is no sin* (essentially and forever).*"* In Christ Jesus, sin does not exist, nor any judgment and condemnation (Romans 8:1). As the children of God, we are the body of Christ, and He is our head. We are to look to Him so we can have the mindset of *"as He is so are we in this world"* (I John 4:12).

Think about what this means, and then think about what really goes on in the church today. How often do we give place to the mindset of being a sinner? If we are *looking* for His appearing then we should *not see* sin in mankind. Jesus did not *see* sin. I repeat; JESUS DID NOT SEE SIN!! He declared the finished work of salvation for all men before the foundations of the world (Jeremiah 1:5). He took back the children of God that the enemy had stolen, declaring them righteous in His sight!

Seeing through the eyes of Christ begins with the understanding of our own identity. It is not our choice to receive Jesus Christ as our personal savior because He already chose to accept us. He, as God, decided our spiritual birth, just as He also decided our natural birth through our natural parents. Our decision is whether or not we acknowledge our true identity as children of God, which was brought back into the Father's presence because of the finished work on the cross. It is also our choice to acknowledge that the life of the flesh that is in the blood of all mankind is the blood of Jesus (Leviticus 17:11). This blood life of God gives everyone the power and authority of the Father. We have the ability to receive our inheritance today versus someday in the future. However, we must be mature in Christ so that when the workings of the Father are done through our flesh, it is His glory that is amplified, not ours.

When a child is born into a royal family, he is raised differently than a common boy or girl. He learns of his position, authority, and power to one day rule as a king. If a child is born of royalty, but kidnapped as a newborn and never raised with the inheritance he legally has, he won't have the confidence in his power and authority that should have been taught to him as a child. Learning of his royalty as an adult will cause confusion, insecurity, and doubt because of the childhood issues he must overcome that would not have been part of being raised as royalty. If there is understanding, love, warmth, and forgiveness from the family because of the mistakes that are made, the person will be an over comer and probably a very good king with understanding and compassion. If, however, the person were met with frustration, judgment, and criticism from the royal family it would be difficult to find the security and confidence to take on the position of a selfless king.

When we are raised in a church environment that is critical, using do's and don'ts to declare Christianity, we are mixing the legalism of religion with the finished work of the cross. It causes a double-minded temple of God, which can't be. The temple of God must only have the mind of God in order for the finished work of Jesus Christ to flow bringing forth the manifestation of His appearing.

Let us go to Matthew 16:13 in the KJV, *"Whom do men say that I the Son of man am?"* In Verse 16 of this chapter we read, *"Thou art the Christ, the Son of the living God."* When Peter declared these words he saw the "appearing" right then. The revelation of the Word was given to him right then and he saw Jesus as He is. In Matt. 16:18 Jesus responds saying, *"Thou art Peter, and upon this rock I will build my church."* Notice that Peter's anointing of revelation did not change him into Jesus. His name is Peter, but he received an anointing of revelation from God. The nugget of revelation in Verse 16 is the stone that builds the church, the body of Jesus Christ.

Let's talk about stones. Stones are used to build with, but they can also come down upon something and destroy. Some people use the phrase, "I received a nugget (something small, but useful or valuable) from the Lord." A nugget is a piece of gold in the form of a rock. God's character is gold and a revelation of Jesus Christ is a rock given by the Holy Spirit. Stones are revelations of the Word of God, Jesus Christ, in manifestation of the Son of God. It is the Word, Jesus Christ, who brought the will of the Father to the world to redeem all mankind giving them Life, Light, and Love. When the Word is revealed in this manifestation, it is building the body of Jesus Christ for His appearing. However, when the Word is used to bind people with rules and condemnation bringing forth the law versus the love of Jesus, then it tears down and destroys.

Is the appearing of Jesus Christ subject to time, or is eternity brought into time to be in this world, but not of this world? Peter saw the "appearing" of Jesus Christ as the Son of God when the Holy Spirit revealed the eternalness of Jesus at that moment in time. The revelation that Peter received was the declaration of a stone, the truth of God's word, being made tangible coming from heaven and being manifested on the earth.

In Daniel 2:34-35 we read of a stone that destroys the mighty image in Nebuchadnezzar's dream. *"Thou sawest till that a stone was cut out without hands, which smote the image upon his feet that were of iron and clay, and broke them to pieces. Then was the iron, the clay, the brass, the silver, and the gold, broken to pieces together, and became like the chaff of the summer threshing floors; and the wind carried them away, that no place was found for them: and the stone that smote the image became a great mountain, and filled the whole earth."* This dream is a representation of how man's imagination can create; the power man has to create through the ability of using his imagination. Even though man may think he is capable of creating awesome and fearsome things, one stone from heaven (one Word) will crush and destroy the creation of man. In Matt. 16:18 Jesus speaks about the gates of hell not prevailing against revelation knowledge, or the rock of God.

Think about the creation of tall buildings, nuclear bombs, huge ocean liners, medical science, etc. Some creations are good and some are not, but all are either of God or of man. If it is of man, then there is the ability by the power of the Word to crush and destroy the creation. All that is left is the "great mountain" of Daniel 2:35, which is the Mount of Olives, or the lives of all men, where Jesus exchanged His righteousness for our sin to do away with sin. It is the mount of unconditional love and forgiveness our Father has for ALL mankind.

In the Amplified Bible, Galatians 1:11-16 says, *"For I want you to know brethren, that the Gospel which was proclaimed and made known by me is not MAN'S GOSPEL* (a human invention, according to or patterned after any human standard). *For indeed I did not receive it from man, nor was I TAUGHT it, but* (it came to me) *through a* (direct) *revelation* (given) *by Jesus Christ* (the Messiah). *You have heard of my earlier career and former manner of life in the Jewish religion* (Judaism), *how I persecuted and abused the church of God furiously and extensively, and* (with fanatical zeal did my best) *to make havoc of it and destroy it. And* (you have heard how) *I outstripped many of the men of my own generation among the people of my race in* (my advancement in study and observance of the laws of) *Judaism, so extremely enthusiastic and zealous I was for the traditions of my ancestors. But when He, Who had chosen and set me apart* (even) *before I was born and called me by His grace* (His undeserved favor and blessing), *saw fit and was pleased to reveal* (unveil, disclose) *His Son within me so that I might proclaim Him among the Gentiles* (non-Jewish world) *as the glad tidings* (Gospel), *immediately I did not confer with flesh and blood* (did not consult or counsel with any frail human being or communicate with anyone)."

Many times these Scripture words are taught with a denominational mindset. I have emphasized a few of the words to emphasize what Scripture says versus what religion says. Think about this in comparison to your religious training. The Amplified Bible is not an alteration of Scripture, but it enhances words of Hebrew and Greek that may have had other meanings than those in the English language.

The Holy Spirit came to Paul and revealed in him all that was truth concerning the Lord Jesus Christ. The teachings that he had been following were those of the great religious leaders or theologians of the day. What they were teaching him, before the Holy Spirit came, was how to be the best Jew by keeping the law and traditions of the faith. He was zealous in setting an example of the Jewish faith. The Holy Spirit showed him that the teachings he had received that he thought were for the means of interacting with God were really benefiting the religious doctrine of the priesthood. Could we ask this same question on our own Christian walk? How often do we use the Word to lift up a doctrine or a denomination versus Jesus? Paul shows us that we can belong to a religious community, be submissive to the law (the Word), and yet be destroying the church of God, the body of Jesus Christ. Paul was a good religious person active in the faith of Judaism, yet he was destroying the body.

When God is involved there is no destruction. When God is being manifested, the stone of the Word builds the body of Jesus Christ. The law will take the Word and bring judgment and condemnation. With the Holy Spirit there will be the manifestation of Jesus, which brings life, healing, wholeness, redemption, and preservation to bring forth the fullness of who He is in His body, which is you and me.

Religion gives us the image of a magical appearing of Jesus Christ; that someday He will appear out of the air instantly. As long as this mindset is being emphasized in the body of Christ we are glorifying the wrong father. There is no building of the church. It is being kept in the bondage of time versus enjoying the inheritance of Life, Love, and Light that is available to us today. Today is the day of our redemption in Christ Jesus. The fullness of our inheritance is within us waiting for us to declare His truth to transform us into His image. Eternity has no yesterdays and no tomorrows. Yesterdays do not exist in eternity and tomorrows are a part of time, not God. The fullness of eternity can only be enjoyed in the NOW. Hebrews 11:1 says, *"Now faith is the substance of things hoped for, the evidence of things NOT seen."*

Let us take a look at Colossians 3:10-14. Verse 10 says, *"Put on the new man, which is renewed in knowledge after the image of him that created him."* Our Son-ship was restored two thousand years ago. Verse 11 says, *"Where there is neither Greek nor Jew, circumcision nor uncircumcision, Barbarian, Scythian, bond nor free: but Christ is ALL, and in ALL."* This is telling us that whether we have a personal relationship with Jesus Christ or not He finished the work of restoration for ALL mankind, and is now in ALL mankind, which transformed the fallen nature of Adam back into the image of God that Adam had in the beginning of creation.

Verses 12-13 says, *"Put on therefore, as the elect of God, holy and beloved, bowels of mercies, kindness, humbleness of mind, meekness, longsuffering; forbearing one another, and forgiving one another, if any man has a quarrel against any; even as Christ forgave you, so also do ye."* Once we have an understanding of the finished work that He did for us on the cross, we have a responsibility as Christians to continue His work with the mindset of Verses 12 and 13. This is a mindset that sees men as brothers and sisters in Christ whether they acknowledge they are Christians or not. It is not up to us to make a decision about another's relationship with the Father. WE are to intercede in their burdens with the forgiveness, kindness, mercy, etc. that has no judgment or condemnation. Verse 14 tells us, *"And above all these things put on charity (love) which is the bond of perfectness."*

Jesus tells us in Matthew 5:44-45, *"But I say unto you, love your enemies, bless them that curse you, do good to them that hate you, and pray for them which despitefully use you, and persecute you; that ye may be the children of your Father which is in heaven: for he maketh his sun to rise on the evil and on the good, and sendeth rain on the just and on the unjust."* Verse 48, *"Be ye therefore perfect even as your Father which is in heaven is perfect."*

When we love with the unconditional love and forgiveness of the Father, who sent Jesus Christ to redeem all mankind back to Him, we see all men through the eyes of God. Matt. 6:22 says, *"The light of the body is the eye; if therefore thine eye be single, thy whole body shall be full of light."* If you only see love and forgiveness in others the way Jesus did with no condemnation (Romans 8:1), then your body is full of the light of God and His love. That light will draw those in spiritual darkness to God. Darkness cannot consume light unless the light is taken out, but light can consume darkness. In Deuteronomy 4:24 and Hebrews 12:29 we are told that God is a consuming fire.

We are taking a life when we misuse the power and authority of the Word bringing judgment and condemnation. The saying, "sticks and stones may break my bones, but words may never harm me" is wrong! It is a lie of the highest order. Proverbs 18:21 tells us that words have the power of life and death.

Going back to Colossians 3:16, we read, *"Let the word of Christ dwell in you richly in all wisdom; teaching and admonishing one another in psalms and hymns and spiritual songs, singing with grace in your hearts to the Lord."* When God's word becomes our word we teach, encourage, and lift others to the Father with the grace, mercy, and praise of our words.

Verse 3:17 says, *"And whatsoever ye do in word or deed, do all in the name of the Lord Jesus, giving thanks to God and the Father by him."* We do not have the right to judge anyone of any sin. We do not have the right to undo the finished work established by Jesus by declaring that some people will go to heaven and some will go to hell.

In closing this chapter, let us read Colossians 1:12-22 from the Amplified Bible, *"Giving thanks unto the Father, which hath made us meet* (able) *to be partakers of the inheritance of the saints in light* (in love)*: Who hath delivered* (already accomplished) *us from the power of darkness* (evil) *and hath translated* (placed) *us into the kingdom* (where God is) *of his dear Son* (his body, soul, and spirit)*: In whom we have redemption* (payment has been made) *through his blood, even the forgiveness of sins: who is the image* (exact likeness) *of the invisible God, the firstborn* (the first of ALL others) *of every creature* (man or beast*): For by him were ALL things created that are in heaven, and that are in earth, visible and invisible, whether they be thrones, or dominions, or principalities, or powers: ALL things were created by him, and for him: And he is before ALL things, and by him ALL things consist. And he is the head of the body, the church: who is the beginning, the firstborn from the dead; that in ALL things he might have the preeminence. For it pleased* (fullness of glory) *the Father that in him should ALL fullness* (completeness of time, of all creation) *dwell; and having made peace through the blood of his cross, by him to reconcile* (the restoration of a relationship of peace) *ALL things unto himself; by him, I say, whether they be things in earth, or things in heaven. And you, that were sometimes alienated and enemies in your mind by wicked works, yet NOW hath he reconciled. In the body of his flesh through death, to present you Holy* (body, soul, and spirit*), and unblamable, and unbearable in his sight."*

I have capitalized the "all" word in these Scriptures to encourage the question did God mean "ALL" when He said "all"?

His perfect body, soul, and spirit are our inheritance to receive NOW, so that as others see us they see Him; for He is All in All (I Corinthians 15:28).

8

Bringing Forth the Sons of God

"After this I looked, and behold, a door was opened in heaven. And the first voice which I heard was as it were of a trumpet talking with me; which said, come up hither, and I will show thee things which must be hereafter." (Revelation. 4:1)

Revelation knowledge is the doorway that brings access of heavenly things (the mind of Christ) into the earth (the flesh). In Revelation Chapters 2 and 3, Jesus gives an illustration of seven churches that each have something to overcome in order to enter into heaven or the Holy of Holies. After the overcoming, the first sound that John hears is like a trumpet that has a voice. This voice is a heavenly voice that is telling John to come up. He is immediately in the spirit (the mind of Christ), yet he is still on the earth or in his natural body. He didn't float off somewhere.

Revelation 4:2 tells us that a throne is set in heaven and One sat on the throne. Heaven is in us and the great white throne of judgment is our heart where God is. He is where His kingdom would be of righteousness, peace, and joy in the Holy Ghost. John is experiencing the Holy of Holies as described in the Old Testament of the Tabernacle in the wilderness within himself. Jesus is the door (John 10:9). In the Old Testament, the temple that God resided in was outside of man, but on the earth. Jesus brought the kingdom of God to reside within man (earth) when He breathed on the disciples and said, *"Peace BE unto (into) you; as my Father hath sent me, even so send I you"* (John 20-21).

Jesus is showing John that the veil, which separated the people from the presence of God, is now torn giving us the ability to manifest the life of Christ while in our bodies. We no longer need to look out there somewhere for God, but to find His throne within ourselves. The church must give acknowledgement to recognizing their true identity and power of being the light, or the Sons of God, as Adam was (Luke 3:38), and as Jesus is (Matt. 1:1).

In the natural, our bodies are given life by the brain. As Christ ones the Spirit of God in us is what gives life to our spirit, which should be the same mind that is in Christ Jesus (Phil. 2:5). In the mind of Christ we acknowledge that the *"Word is truth, and we are sanctified through truth"* (John 17:17). The issue is not when something will happen, because God is not subject to time. By faith, we believe it is already done in the heavens whether we see it or not. On earth, we need to acknowledge the completion of the finished work by faith for the manifestation to take place, subject to His timing, in the earth.

On the day of Calvary, the veil was rent from the top to the bottom (Matthew 27:51). Heaven was brought to earth affecting ALL of creation including the dead in the graves. In order for transformation of the body of Christ to be manifested, the sons of God must begin with a changed mind rather than camping at the foot of the cross, never getting beyond being a "sinner saved by grace." In Ephesians 2:4-6 we are told, *"But God, who is rich in mercy, for his great love wherewith he loved us, even when we were dead in sins, hath quickened us together with Christ, and hath raised us up together, and made us sit together in heavenly places in Christ Jesus."* The word "hath" is a finished or completed word. The word "together" is a corporate word that encompasses "all" which took place at one point in time. We have "all" been made alive from our sins, raised from the dead, and are now sitting together with Christ Jesus with the Father.

To be carnally minded brings judgment and condemnation that in turn brings destruction and death (Romans 8:6). Yet, *"There is no condemnation to them that are in Christ Jesus"* (Romans 8:1). To be in Christ Jesus we have His mind, which is His life and peace (Romans 8:1-11). Jesus is the head, the mind or the husband. We are the flesh and bone, the body, the wife, and/or the woman.

If we ponder each of these words found in Scripture to describe us, we should think on their eternal expansion versus the temporal or literal significance. For example, the bones of Jesus are not to be broken signifies his body, flesh, or woman (bride). The garment He wore was not to be rent apart for His garment has no beginning and no end. This garment is righteousness of the saints (Revelation 19:8), which can't be taken away because there is no beginning or end. Jesus is the alpha and omega. The body of Christ is known as the "earth." In 2 Peter 3:13 we read of, *"a new earth, where in dwelleth righteousness."* The veil of the natural temple had to be torn from top to bottom to signify the finished work of the natural, and the doors opened to the heavens, the Holy of Holies on the earth.

God is perfecting a many member body to be manifested on this earth as the Sons of God. He that has the Son has the Father (Galatians 1:16). As they see the Son, they see the Father (John 14:10)...Selah.

If you have the mind of God, then everything you look at should be with perfection (Heb. 4:1-4). *"It is not what goes into the mouth that defileth a man; but that which cometh out of the mouth, this defileth a man"* (Matt. 15:11). The mouth has the ability to produce life or death by our words (Prov. 18:21). When we speak by faith, with the voice of our Father, we produce life.

When we speak His word without faith, adding emotions of doubt or insecurity of what He has said, we take the "butt" that God created to be behind us and place it on our face. I know this sounds disgusting, yet that is how dramatic it is when we have the "see it to believe it" mentality. We bring legalism, judgment, and death to what is supposed to produce life (Rev. 22:18-19).

Some thoughts to ponder:

"We have been created in His Image, after His kind." (Gen. 1:26)

"Our heart's cry should be that the words of our mouth and the meditations of our hearts be acceptable to Him." (Psalms 19:14)

"As others see me, they would see the Son, they would see the Father." (John 17:21-23)

"Who (God) will have all men to be saved and to come unto the knowledge of the truth. For there is one God and one mediator between God and men, the man Christ Jesus." (1 Timothy 2:4-5)

"For this reason, we labor and suffer reproach, because we trust in the living God, who is the Savior of all men, especially of those that believe." (1 Timothy 4:10)

"That you may be blameless and harmless, the Sons of God without rebuke, in the midst of a crooked and perverse nation, among whom you shine as lights in the world." (Phil. 2:15)

"For God is light, and in Him there is no darkness at all." (1 John 1:5)

9

Being Transformed into His Image

"And be not conformed to this world: but be ye transformed by the renewing of your mind, that ye may prove what is that good, and acceptable, and perfect, will of God." Romans 12:2

"For who hath known the mind of the Lord that he may instruct him? But we have the mind of Christ." I Corinthians 2:16

The word "transformed" used in the Scripture above is more than just the process of thinking differently. This word in the Greek means "metamorphoo" in which we get our English word "metamorphous." The prefix "meto" denotes change of condition, and "morphoo" means to form.

This is the same word used with Jesus at the Mount of Transfiguration found in Matthew 17:2 and Mark 9:2. This word "transformed" involves the miracle of going from an earthly form into a supernatural form. The word itself can be broken into "trans" meaning to go beyond or above, and "form" which relates to the physical body or world. In the book of Romans 12:2, Paul is telling us to be transformed, or go beyond the limits of our natural body, soul, and mind into the supernatural or spirit realm. How do we do this? The verse further tells us it is done by the renewing of our minds with the knowing and confirming in our spirit that we have the mind of Christ. Why would we desire to be transformed? According to the word of the Lord, it would be for the good, acceptable, and perfect will of God to be manifested in us. I believe that if God has told us to do this, then it must be a goal we can obtain within ourselves while alive in our natural bodies.

When we allow our minds to be renewed into the mind of Christ; our spirit, soul, and body will begin to transform into His image. We can begin this transformation process when we change our thoughts and the words we speak into, "What would Jesus say or do in this situation?"

Proverbs 23:7 says, *"For as a man thinketh in his heart, so is he: Eat and drink, saith he to thee; but his heart is not with thee."* This Scripture is telling us that what we experience with our senses about someone (the way they look, smell, talk, or act) may not be what is really going on within them. It may be a cover-up to play the game of life the world expects us to reflect, but inside there may be major turmoil going on that is being hidden.

In the book of Mark, Chapter 7, Verses 15-23, Jesus gives us a teaching about what comes from the heart.

"There is nothing from without a man that entering into him can defile him: but the things which come out of him, those are they that defile the man. If any man have ears to hear let him hear. And when he was entered in the house from the people, his disciples asked him con-

cerning the parable. And he saith unto them, Are ye so without understanding also? Do ye not perceive, that whatsoever thing from without entereth into the man, it cannot defile him; because it entereth not into his heart, but into the belly, and goeth out into the draught, purging all meats? And he said, that which cometh out of the man, that defileth the man. For from within, out of the heart of men, proceed evil thoughts, adulteries, fornications, murders, thefts, covetousness, wickedness, deceit, lasciviousness, an evil eye, blasphemy, pride, foolishness: All these evil things come from within, and defile the man."

The following are suggestions of helpful ways to begin transforming from a child of God, who seeks self-desires, into a Son of God, who is doing the Father's business. These suggestions are only a beginning and not the full process of manifestation. Our Heavenly Father is eternal, and His ways never end, therefore we must anticipate a new beginning of transformation to take place each day that is not limited by time or space. With God, our objective should be to manifest peace in the midst of the journey of life versus trying to hang on to the finish line of death and getting to heaven someday. When there is peace in the middle of trials and tribulations there will be a manifestation of timeless patience brought by faith, thus producing hope and contentment (Romans 5:3-4). When we allow the mind of Christ to be in control of the situation, we are connecting to God where there is no time involved. Without time, everything exists in "NOW" which by faith is completed or finished.

The Amplified Bible tells us, *"Now Faith is the assurance* (the confirmation, the title deed) *of the things* (we) *hope for, being the proof of things* (we) *do not see and the conviction of their reality* (faith perceiving as real fact what is not revealed to the senses)."

1. *We must seek first the Kingdom of God,* which is righteousness, peace, and joy in the Holy Ghost (Romans 14:17). This kingdom is not floating out in space, but is within you (Luke 17:21). If you have a choice of seeking peace or being right, seek peace instead of justification. With peace, true righteousness will follow in the Father's timing.

2. *Love the Lord God with ALL your heart, soul, mind, and strength.* This is given by Jesus in Mark 12:30 as the first commandment. When you give ALL there is no self-identity left. Jesus refers to this as act of intimacy to where there is covenant exchange. We can find the natural parallel to this verse in the bedroom of a couple's wedding night, and they are both virgins giving of themselves in intimacy connected with intercourse. The next morning they are no longer independent in their identity, but have joined their body, soul, and spirit to become one. When we enter this covenant exchange with Jesus Christ, all that we were before we came to know Him personally, and all that He is now, becomes one within us.

3. *Desire to grow up from a child stage of Christianity.* This stage is more concerned with what "benefits" one can receive from being in the family of God than being like Jesus. Children have a "me" mentality desiring recognition from others to build them up, versus seeking within themselves the supernatural power and identity that is already theirs to give away to others with no "self" involved. An example of a

child stage of Christianity is, "Woe is me, a poor sinner saved by grace, not worthy to be in the family of God." Though this may sound humble, it is very much egotistical. This mindset is saying God doesn't really have full control of creation, and that the finished work of Calvary isn't enough to redeem mankind. Even though Scripture tells us God is ALL in ALL (I Corinthians 15:28). The greatest fear the "child" Christian has is the responsibility to grow up to do the Father's business. It is difficult to let go of self-control and allow the Holy Spirit to be in charge. However, when we do, there is a peace that surpasses all of our natural mind's understanding, allowing the love of our Heavenly Father to flow in us, and transform us into His image. Most Christians profess to be in the family of God but believe they will receive their inheritance after they die, which gives them an excuse of not being able to do the Father's business today. The Father's pattern of life was never to produce children out of wedlock. In order for transformation to occur and the fruit of covenant exchange to be manifested, we cannot just talk about what takes place in the bedroom on a wedding night, but be willing to exchange our lives for His today. In the natural, children cannot be created without the seed of the man impregnating the woman through intercourse. In the spirit, we must exchange our lives on the cross of Calvary for His resurrected life allowing the breath that He breathed on the disciples in John 20:21 to be the breath of the Holy Spirit in us for the fruit in Galatians 5:22 to be manifested. We can't give away what we don't have to give. Little children don't produce children. There must be a growth process to a stage of maturity for reproduction to occur. To go forth and multiply spiritually, as Adam and Eve were commanded to bring forth more children in His image, we must know we possess His image to give to others.

4. After we have exchanged covenants with Jesus Christ as described in Galatians 2:20, then in Mark 12:31, Jesus tell us the next commandment for us to do is to *love thy neighbor as thyself.* We must see and love others the way our Heavenly Father has loved us, sending Jesus Christ to die for us while we were still in a rebellious state of separation from the love of God (Romans 5:8). There is no greater love than to lay down your life for another as Jesus did for us (John 15:13).

5. *Let go of the past.* If the past doesn't bring the fruits of the Holy Spirit into your present, then let it go or else it will bring contamination into the purity of the love of God in you. This includes forgiving yourself and others with an unconditional forgiveness. It does not mean that you have to accept the wrong, or even confront the person if it will cause further conflict. However, it does mean that you have to let go of the situation with unconditional forgiveness, allowing God to bring healing to both you and the other person. We do not know the circumstances of a person's past that lead them to be involved in a situation, or to say words of hurt or abuse. When we look beyond our natural eyes and see Jesus in "misfit" circumstances, we are able to allow the Holy Spirit to bring healing and unity to both ourselves and the other people involved. This is one reason

God gives us time to allow the process of forgiveness to take place.

6. *Any judgment or condemnation of thought or deed towards another must be managed within ourselves penetrating to our heart.* Romans 8:1 says, *"There is therefore NOW no condemnation to them which are in Christ Jesus who walk not after the flesh, but after the Spirit."* Many times we don't really deal with it, but cover it up until something in our life triggers the remembrance of the past hurt. Then the situation we thought we had let go comes rushing back into our thoughts like a spark that quickly turns into a burning house. Not only must we give it to Jesus, but we must also count it all joy with blessings to give away. Our Heavenly Father judges no man (John 5:22). He gave the execution of ALL judgment to Jesus, which He completed at Calvary over two thousand years ago (John 5:27). We are told in Matthew 7:1-2 that we are not to judge, but if we do, then that same judgment or condemnation we placed on the other person, whether in thought, word, or deed, will happen to us. It may not happen immediately, but our words are not limited to time. On the same scale, if we bring unconditional love, peace, and forgiveness to another, the same will be returned to us. Again, we may not see it immediately, or in the same form, but by faith in God's word there will be blessings that will come about in His timing. In James 1:2-4 we read, *"My brethren, count it all joy when ye fall into divers temptations; knowing this, that the trying of your faith worketh patience. But let patience have her perfect work, that ye may be perfect and entire, wanting nothing."* We have a choice with each

positive or negative in our life, to see them as the schoolmaster of teaching us maturity in Christ, or to stay as a child spiritually. True son-ship is to see that our purpose in this world is not about "me," but to bring glory and honor to the Father.

7. *Walk in the Spirit of God* allowing the fruit of the Holy Spirit to be manifested from within you for others to see. These fruits are: love, joy, peace, longsuffering, gentleness, goodness, faith, meekness, and temperance (Galatians 5:16, 22-26). All of these are based on the unconditional love, mercy, and forgiveness we can only give away as we allow ourselves to receive the fullness of our Father's inheritance that Jesus gave us from his resurrection on the third day. Once we allow "condition" to enter into the circumstance, we bring "feelings" which also remove faith. This takes God out of control in our life bringing "ego" in to authority. *"But the hour cometh, and NOW IS when true worshipers shall worship the Father in spirit and in truth* (Jesus): *for the Father seeketh such to worship him. God is a spirit: and they that worship him must worship in spirit and in truth"* (John 4:23-24).

8. *"Follow peace with ALL, and holiness, without no man shall see the Lord"* (Hebrews 12:14). We must strive to go up to a higher calling to allow the peace of God, which goes beyond the realms of our natural understanding to come forth. In doing so Matthew 5:9 of the Amplified Bible tells us, *"Blessed* (enjoying enviable happiness, spiritually prosperous with life-joy and satisfaction in God's favor and salvation,

regardless of their outward conditions) *are the makers and maintainers of peace, for they shall be called the sons of God!"*

9. *Change your thoughts to change the world around you.* "*Finally, brethren, whatsoever things are true, whatsoever things are honest, whatsoever things are just, whatsoever things are pure, whatsoever things are lovely, whatsoever things are of good report; if there be any virtue, and if there be any praise, think on these things*" (Philippians 4:8). If we allow ourselves to be a witness to our thoughts, and be willing to change our vocabulary from negative thoughts, doubts, and/or fears into positives we can open doors to being able to count it all joy. We can either see the circumstances around us as the "cup is half full getting fuller" or the "cup is half empty and going dry." We are not bodies with a spirit, but have been created as a spirit with a soul, mind, emotions, and personality being made in the image of our Heavenly Father out of pure love, residing in a body.

Let us find stillness so that we may know (intimacy of spiritual intercourse) God (Psalm 46:10). In doing so the joy of the Lord will be your strength (Nehemiah 8:10), allowing us to be transformed into His image. May our Heavenly Father's blessing and love be upon you, lifting you into His presence, and into a higher calling for your life.

A Thought to Keep You Teachable

Have you ever questioned where the people that came out of the grave in Matthew 27 went after Jesus rose from the dead? They couldn't die again. How about Lazarus being brought out of the grave after three days? He truly died once, so he couldn't die again. This would really go against the Scripture that says, *"It is appointed unto man once to die and then the judgment"* (Hebrews 9:27). The judgment is the mercy seat of God declaring they are alive and complete in Him which is the head (Colossians 2:10), but where did they go after they rose and walked on the earth and ate with the mortals? Yes, Lazarus did eat with Jesus and the Disciples after he came out of the grave!

(Sounds like a good rabbit trail to write another book!)

APPENDIX

Bringing Forth the Sons of God

❖

According to the Word of the Lord

The following are Scriptures that will be an encouragement for you to step out of your comfort zone of traditional teachings on Christianity. As I began my research, the word "ALL" began to stand out bringing me to ask the Father, if "all" really meant "ALL." The Holy Spirit challenged me with the question, "How big is your faith to want to believe that "all" really means "ALL"? The extent of your faith is what will determine "ALL" in your life. It was then that the Lord reminded me that, "I could do ALL things through Christ which strengthened me." (Philippians 4:13)

These Scriptures have been taken from the King James Version of the Bible. The parenthesis are mine, along with capitalizing the word "ALL" to help you reconsider the way you may have been interpreting our Father's love letters in the past.

"Which was the son of Enos, which was the son of Seth, which was the son of Adam, which was the Son of God." (Luke 3:38)

"In the day that God created man, in the likeness (image) *of God* (himself) *made he him: Male and female* (both Adam) *created he them; and blessed them, and called their name Adam, in the day when they were created."* (Genesis 5:1-2)

"And in thee shall ALL families of the earth be blessed." (Genesis 12:3)

"The Lord is gracious, and full of compassion; slow to anger, and of great mercy. The Lord is good to ALL: and his tender mercies are over ALL his works. ALL thy works shall praise thee, O Lord; and thy saints shall bless thee." (Psalm 145:8-10)

"For since by man came death, by man came also the resurrection of the dead. For as in Adam ALL die, even so in Christ shall ALL be made alive." (I Corinthians 15:21-22)

"For it is God which worketh in you both to will and to do of his good pleasure." (Philippians 2:13)

"Do ALL things without murmurings and disputing: That ye may be blameless and harmless, the sons of God, without rebuke, in the midst of a crooked and perverse nation, among whom ye shine as lights in the world." (Philippians 2:14-15)

"Let this mind be in you, which was also in Christ Jesus: Who, being in the form of God, thought it not robbery to be equal with God." (Philippians 2:5-6)

"For the Father judgeth no man, but hath committed all judgment unto the Son." (John 5:22)

"Verily, verily, I say unto you, the Son can do nothing of himself, but what he seeth the Father do: for what things soever he doeth, these also doeth the Son likewise." (John 5:19)

"ALL things were made by him; and without him was not any thing made that was made. In him was life: and the life was the light of men." (John 1:3-4)

"But as many as received him to them gave he power to become the sons of God, even to them that believe on him name." (John 1:12)

"Jesus saith unto them, 'My meat is to do the will of him that sent me, and to finish his work.'" (John 4:34)

"The Lord is not slack concerning his promise, as some men count slackness; but is longsuffering to us-ward, not willing that any should perish, but that ALL should come to repentance." (2 Peter 3:9)

"Not by the works of righteousness which we have done, but according to his mercy he saved us, by the washing of regeneration, and renewing of the Holy Ghost; which he shed on us abundantly through Jesus Christ our Savior; that being justified by his grace, we should be made heirs according to the hope of eternal life." (Titus 3: 5-7)

"Therefore as by the offense of one judgment came upon ALL men to condemnation; even so by the righteousness of one the free gift came upon ALL men unto justification of life." (Romans 5:18)

"There is therefore now no condemnation to them which are in Christ Jesus who walk not after the flesh, but after the Spirit." (Romans 8:1)

"For I am persuaded, that neither death, nor life, nor angels, nor principalities, nor powers, nor things present, nor things to come, nor height, nor depth, nor any other creature, shall be able to separate us from the love of God, which is in Christ Jesus our Lord." (Romans 8:38-39)

"Know ye not that ye are the temple of God, and that the Spirit of God dwelleth in you?" (I Corinthians 3:16)

"Let no man glory in men, For ALL things are yours; whether Paul, or Apollos, or Cephas, or the world, or life, or death, or things present, or things to come; ALL are yours; And ye are Christ's, and Christ is God's." (I Corinthians 3:21-23)

"For by him were ALL things created, that are in heaven, and that are in earth, visible and invisible, whether they be thrones, or dominions, or principalities, or powers: ALL things were created by him, and for him: and he is before ALL things, and by him ALL things consist." (Colossians 1:16-17)

"And hath made of one blood ALL nations of men for to dwell on all the face of the earth, and hath determined the times before appointed, and the abounds of their habitation; that they should seek the Lord, if haply they might feel after him, and find him, though he be not far from every one of us: for in him we live, and move, and have our being; as certain also of your own poets have said, For we are also his offspring." (Acts 17:26-28)

"Therefore if any man be in Christ, he is a new creature: old things are passed away; behold ALL things are become new. And ALL things are of God, who hath reconciled us to himself by Jesus Christ, and hath given to us the ministry of reconciliation." (2 Corinthians 5:17-18)

"I am crucified with Christ: nevertheless I live; yet not I, but Christ liveth in me: and the life which I now live in the flesh I live by the faith of the Son of God, who loved me, and gave himself for me." (Galatians 2:20)

"And if ye be Christ's, then are ye Abraham's seed, and heirs according to the promise." (Galatians 3:29)

"And because ye are sons, God hath sent forth the Spirit of his Son into your hearts, crying Abba, Father." (Galatians 4:6)

"Verily, verily, I say unto you, if a man keeps my saying, he shall never see death." (John 8:51)

"Jesus answered them, 'Is not written in your law, I said ye are gods?'" (John 10:34)

"Now is the judgment of this world: now shall the prince of this world be cast out. And I if I be lifted up from the earth will draw ALL men unto me. This he said, signifying what death he should die." (John 12:31-33)

"Therefore, leaving the principles of the doctrine of Christ, let us go on unto perfection; laying again the foundation of repentance from dead works, and of faith toward God, of the doctrine of baptisms, and of laying on of hands, and of resurrection of the dead, and of eternal judgment." (Hebrews 6:1-2)

"We know that we have passed from death unto life, because we love the brethren. He that loveth not his brother abideth in death." (1 John 3:14)

"Ye are of God, little children, and have overcome them: because greater is he that is in you, than he that is in the world." (1 John 4:4)

"Beloved, let us love one another: for love is of God; and every one that loveth is born of God, and knoweth God." (1 John 4:7)

"That which was from the beginning, which we have heard, which we have seen with our eyes, which we have looked upon, and our hands have handled, of the Word of life." (1 John 1:1)

"And these things write we unto you, that your joy may be full. This then is the message which we have heard of him, and declare unto you, that God is light, and in him is no darkness at ALL." (1 John 1:4-5)

"Then Jesus said unto them, 'Yet a little while is the light with you. Walk while ye have the light, lest darkness come upon you: for he that walketh in darkness knoweth not whither he goeth. While ye have light, believe in the light, that ye may be the children of light.'" (John 12:35-36)

"Ye have not chosen me, but I have chosen you, and ordained you, that ye should go and bring forth fruit, and that your fruit should remain: that whatsoever ye shall ask of the Father in my name, he may give it you." (John 15:16)

"Ye are the light of the world. A city that is set on a hill cannot be hid. Let your light so shine before men, that they may see your good works, and glorify your Father which is in heaven." (Matthew 5:14, 16)

"Blessed are the pure in heart: for they shall see God. Blessed are the peacemakers: for they shall be called the children of God." (Matthew 5:8-9)

"Be careful for nothing, but in every thing by prayer and supplication with thanksgiving let your requests by made known unto God. And the peace of God, which passeth all understanding, shall keep your hearts and minds through Christ Jesus. Finally, brethren, whatsoever things are true, whatsoever things are honest, whatsoever things are just, whatsoever things are pure, whatsoever things are lovely, whatsoever thing are of good report; if there be any virtue, and if there be any praise, think on these things." (Philippians 3:6-8)

"Rejoice in the Lord always; and again I say, Rejoice." (Philippians 3:4)

0-595-31244-6